Horribly★FAMOUS

SIR FRANCIS
DRAKE
and his Daring Deeds

by Andrew Donkin

Illustrated by Clive Goddard

Scholastic Children's Books,
Euston House, 24 Eversholt Street,
London NW1 1DB, UK

A division of Scholastic Ltd
London ~ New York ~ Toronto ~ Sydney ~ Auckland
Mexico City ~ New Delhi ~ Hong Kong

First published in the UK by Scholastic Ltd, 2006
This edition published 2012

Text © Andrew Donkin, 2006
Illustrations © Clive Goddard, 2006

ISBN 978 1407 12415 5

Printed and bound by CPI Group (UK) Ltd, Croydon, CR0 4YY

2 4 6 8 10 9 7 5 3 1

The right of Andrew Donkin and Clive Goddard to be identified as the
author and illustrator of this work respectively has been asserted by them
in accordance with the Copyright, Designs and Patents Act, 1988.

Papers used by Scholastic Children's Books are made from woods grown in
sustainable forests.

CONTENTS

Introduction   5

Hello sailor   8

Disaster at sea   20

How to steal a million   31

The age of discovery   44

All aboard   54

Island of blood   66

Where no (English) man   72
has gone before

Stormy weather   80

The dragon   90

The Drake mystery   100

The homeward bounders   107

Drake in command   114

The dragon breathes fire   126

Invasion!   141

On the rocks   154

Last voyages   164

INTRODUCTION

Sir Francis Drake is horribly famous for his daring deeds on the high seas. He's been horribly famous for over 400 years and his real life reads like an amazing adventure story. Nearly everyone knows something about him.

HIS ENEMIES WERE SO SCARED OF HIM THEY CALLED HIM 'THE DRAGON'

Not that everyone was a fan...

KING PHILIP OF SPAIN

HE ROBBED ME BLIND!

Lots of people think they know about Sir Francis Drake, but did you also know that...
• Drake was actually a pirate
• He was fearless, brave, and very greedy
• He flirted with the queen of England

WELL, HE WAS RATHER DASHING!

QUEEN ELIZABETH I

- He chopped the head off one of his own men
- He dined on penguins and alligators (not together!)

- And that he saved England from invasion ... not once, but twice.

This book gives you the lowdown on Drake's amazing life and his incredible three-year voyage around the globe. He was a man of action, and what he did changed the world in which he lived, and shaped the world we live in today.

You can turn to the action-packed pages of *The Daily Drake* for sensational sixteenth-century news reports about the adventures of our boy, and follow his voyages on marvellous sea maps. You'll also learn how to be a pirate and turn a tidy profit, and take an exclusive peek at the sea captain's own secret logbooks. (So secret even he didn't know about them.)

Now it's time to batten down the hatches and hoist the main brace, as we set sail on one of the greatest real-life adventure stories ever...

HELLO SAILOR

No one knows exactly when Francis Drake was born.

SHALL I WRITE OUT A BIRTH CERTIFICATE AND KEEP IT SAFE JUST IN CASE HE GOES ON TO BECOME HORRIBLY FAMOUS AND SAVE ENGLAND FROM INVASION?

IT'S NOT EXACTLY LIKELY IS IT? HE'S JUST A BIG BABY.

WAAA!

Most people who study history, however, agree that our boy Drake was probably born in 1540, in either February or March. Drake's dad was called Edmund Drake; we don't even know his mum's first name, only that she was part of the Myllwaye family. We do know where he was born though. Francis Drake made his debut in the world on Crowndale Farm in Devon, about 15 miles north of Plymouth on the south coast of England.

The Drake family had been living in the area for at least 100 years. In the past the family had been tenant farmers – that meant that they rented the land where they lived and grew crops on it.

Edmund Drake seems to have had several occupations. For many years he worked as a shearman – a skilled craftsman who helped make clothes – and after that he became a priest. The Drakes didn't have a lot of money, but they weren't poor either. They were part of what was called the yeomen class (sort of like the middle class today). They rented some land, but they would have worked that land themselves.

If everyone were included, then a family portrait of the Drake family would have looked something like this:

The Drake Family

9

Including our own Francis, Edmund and his wife went on to have 12 children! (No wonder she looks tired in the picture.) People tended to have a lot more children in those days because, frankly, not all of them would live long enough to grow up. We only know the names of Francis and four of his brothers.

Drake's world
So what was daily life like when Francis Drake was a kid over 400 years ago?

HOME - STONE FARMHOUSE HEATED BY ONE CENTRAL FIRE.

FOOD - LOTS OF IT BUT NOTHING FANCY (UNLESS YOU WERE RICH). BREAD, PARSNIPS, TURNIPS, CARROTS, MILK, CHEESE, FRUIT (PICKED LOCALLY).

CLOTHES - BOYS WERE DRESSED EXACTLY LIKE THEIR DADS FROM ABOUT THE AGE OF SIX. MOST PEOPLE HAD JUST ONE CHANGE OF CLOTHES AND THEY RARELY HAD A BATH (SO THINGS COULD GET QUITE PONGY).

TOILETS DIDN'T EXIST SO YOU DID YOUR ER... DOINGS IN A BUCKET AND CHUCKED IT OUTSIDE ON TO A 'MUCKHILL' LATER.

When Drake was a kid there were only 3.5 million people in the whole of England. That's compared with about 50 million people who live in England today. One reason there were so few people was that they kept getting killed by the plague. Diseases were a big problem on land AND (as we'll see) at sea.

I do like to be beside the seaside

When Francis was eight or nine years old his father moved from Devon, leaving his family behind. He travelled to Kent in southeast England where he became the curate of a village called Upchurch. Upchurch was near the River Medway where lots of Royal Navy ships were docked. Some people think that young Francis went with his dad, but we don't know for sure.

Certainly when he was much older Francis Drake used to enjoy telling stories of his humble (i.e. poor and smelly) background. One of the stories included the time that he and his old dad lived in the hull of an abandoned ship on the river. A lot of people think this is no more than an old sailor's yarn though.

The truth is much more interesting. In those days it was common for parents to send their children to work or

11

serve in the households of relatives who were better off (i.e. not so poor or smelly). The deal worked like this: the child would do some work or service in exchange for which they would be looked after and educated. The Drakes had some well-off relatives in the form of the Hawkins family of Plymouth.

So who were the Hawkins family then?

I'm glad you asked, because they are very important to our story. The head of the Hawkins family was old William Hawkins, who was a merchant and also … well, a bit of a pirate. He had sailed to both Brazil and Africa in his youth, as well as raiding a few French and Spanish ships when he could. William Hawkins made a good living as a merchant (buying things in one country and selling them for more cash in another) who did a little bit of piracy on the side.

Living in the Hawkins household, Francis would have heard everyday talk of far-off exotic countries and their peoples. He would have been told exciting and wonderful stories about old William's adventures capturing Spanish ships and even about the old scoundrel's time in prison as a result.

12

William had two sons of his own, the imaginatively named William and the slightly more imaginatively named John. He was bringing up both boys in the family tradition of seafaring. It is very likely that Francis (along with a couple of his many brothers) spent much of his childhood with the Hawkins boys, learning about the ocean and getting his sea legs.

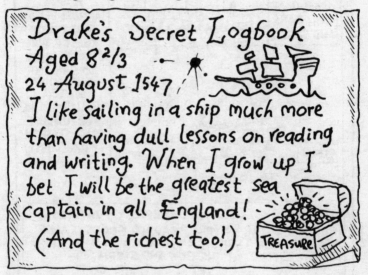

Drake's Secret Logbook
Aged 8²/₃
24 August 1547
I like sailing in a ship much more than having dull lessons on reading and writing. When I grow up I bet I will be the greatest sea captain in all England!
(And the richest too!)
TREASURE

Learning the ropes

So what would young Francis have been taught?

The Hawkins family owned several ships, and there's no doubt that our boy would have got lots of practical experience. He'd have learned to watch the weather and spot when a storm was blowing in. He would have been taught to judge the ebb and flow of the daily tides and learned how they changed over the course of a year. He would have learned how to handle a ship, and something else just as important, how to handle its crew.

Drake's day

Here's a quick guide to the kinds of ships that our boy Drake would have seen...

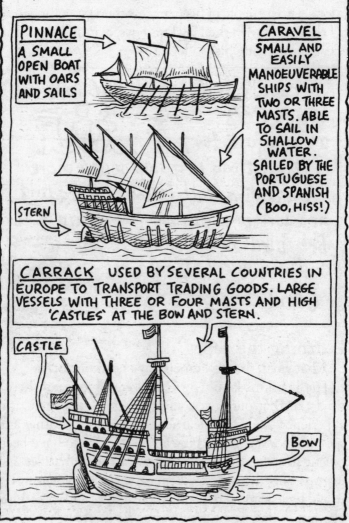

PINNACE
A SMALL OPEN BOAT WITH OARS AND SAILS

CARAVEL
SMALL AND EASILY MANOEUVERABLE SHIPS WITH TWO OR THREE MASTS. ABLE TO SAIL IN SHALLOW WATER. SAILED BY THE PORTUGUESE AND SPANISH (BOO, HISS!)

STERN

CARRACK USED BY SEVERAL COUNTRIES IN EUROPE TO TRANSPORT TRADING GOODS. LARGE VESSELS WITH THREE OR FOUR MASTS AND HIGH 'CASTLES' AT THE BOW AND STERN.

CASTLE

BOW

GALLEON VERY LARGE MULTI-DECKED VESSEL DESIGNED FOR LONG OCEAN VOYAGES. HAS THREE TO FIVE MASTS. GALLEONS WERE DEVELOPED FROM CARRACKS AND CARAVELS AND USED BY BOTH THE ENGLISH AND SPANISH.

Setting sail

We don't know exactly when Drake first went to sea. Certainly by the time he was in his mid-teens he was working on a ship making regular crossings from England to France and Holland. The ship doubtless belonged to the Hawkins family. Drake was clever, able and hard-working. Soon he found himself going further afield.

Drake's Secret Logbook
21 July 1555

me looking good →

Ha! Here I am bound for adventure at last. I am on a ship called the Tiger and I have been made purser – which means I am in charge of pay and supplies. The Tiger is about 50 tons in size and handles well except in high winds. (I wish the captain would let me help. I would do a much <u>much</u> better job.) We will search for French merchant ships to raid, and bring their cargos back to England.

PS - Sounds a bit like piracy, but of course it's not! We are 'privateers', which means that we only pick on ships from other countries. (Naughty countries.) It also means that we hath a licence from Queen Mary saying that we are doing this in her service.

PPS We don't actually have a licence from the Queen, but we could probably get one if we asked. (Maybe.) Which as everyone knows is pretty much the same thing.

Old William Hawkins died in 1555, leaving his two sons to run the family business. William Jr managed the business on land while John became its executive manager on the high seas. It was a combination that worked well, and it was good news for Drake. His natural skills for sailing and navigating had been spotted at an early age, and the fact that he was a relative too meant he could be trusted.

Just a few years later, something happened that was to change the England Drake lived in for ever. Queen Mary popped her clogs and the country suddenly had a new ruler…

THE DAILY DRAKE
Special Coronation Edition 17 January 1559

QUEEN OF ENGLAND!

Yes, England has a new queen! Twenty-five-year-old right-royal redhead, Elizabeth Tudor was today crowned Queen of England, taking the title Queen Elizabeth I.

The carrot-topped charmer thrilled crowds throughout London as her coronation procession travelled towards Westminster Abbey. Punters ignored the icy weather as they crammed the brightly decorated streets to catch a glimpse of their new monarch.

THE DAILY DRAKE says: England has a new queen and let's hope she does better than the last one! Old Queen Mary has left England in a right mess, drained of money, men and arms. We are surrounded by the military might of big boys France and Spain. If Queen Lizzy shows any weakness they'll be ready to pounce.

We say: 'Good luck your majesty.' (You're gonna need it.)

17

Rough seas ahead

No one knew what the future might hold under the new queen. When she came to the throne Elizabeth described England as being in 'a sad state', and she was right. Someone else described England as a country of unemployed people 'wandering idly up and down'. The government had run out of money and, without cash to pay her army and navy, how was Queen Lizzy supposed to protect her kingdom (and herself)?

A tale of two religions

As well as money problems there was the thorny issue of religion. When Drake was growing up, which religion you were was often a matter of life and death. Europe was divided into two types of Christians – Catholics and Protestants. The two sides had been incredibly cruel to each other over the years with plenty of people beheaded or burned at the stake for their beliefs. Drake doubtless saw some of this for himself as a child.

The old queen, Queen Mary, had been a Catholic, but the new queen, Queen Lizzy, was a Protestant. Being the Protestant queen of a country that included a lot of Catholics (as well as Protestants) meant that Lizzy had to be very careful not to upset people.

If Queen Lizzy had written a 'To Do' list on her first day as queen then it would have looked something like this:

1 Make the Protestant Church of England the main church again, but let Catholics do their own thing in private. Result - no one upset. V. good.

2 Avoid war with Spain or France. Do this by pretending I might marry into one side or the other but never do it. Result - no one upset. V. good.

3 Get some cash from somewhere. (V. urgent.)

Meanwhile, down in Plymouth, Francis Drake was rapidly rising through the ranks onboard the Hawkins shipping fleet. Little did Drake realize it, but it wouldn't be too many years before our boy Francis, the son of a humble farmer-turned-preacher, was going to help out Queen Lizzy in a big way and save the entire country. First though, there was going to be a little bit of blood, death and downright disaster.

DISASTER AT SEA

It didn't start with disaster, of course. It started with a new way of making money when the Hawkins brothers decided to try their hand at the slave trade. Slavery was a dirty and terrible business, but it was also a way of getting very rich very quickly. Spain's new colonies in South America were in desperate need of workers and that created a demand for slaves. Here's how it worked:

The slave trade triangle

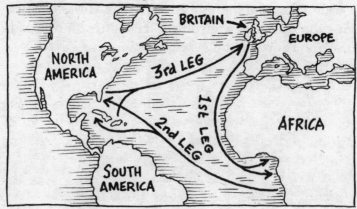

First leg
England to Africa
• Trade English cotton-cloth or other cheap goods for slaves.

Second leg
From Africa across the Atlantic Ocean to the Caribbean or the coast of South America
• Slaves sold to the highest bidder.
• Some of the money is kept as profit; the rest is used to buy goods like hides and sugar.

Third leg
Home to England
• Sell cargo of hides, sugar, etc for large profit.
• A clever captain could make a profit on each leg of the voyage.

The travelling conditions for the slaves were terrible. They were crammed into overcrowded holds with no toilets of any kind, and given very little food and water. No surprise, then, that many poor souls died at sea.

The Hawkins brothers made three major slaving expeditions and Francis Drake sailed on at least two of them. It wasn't that our hero was keen on slavery – he wasn't. But then he wasn't against it either. It seems strange and outrageous today, but in Drake's day slavery was part of daily life. An Englishman caught by the Spanish, for example, was very likely to spend the rest of his life shovelling dirt as a slave in a mine or getting blisters manning the oars of a Spanish ship.

Drake probably made his first voyage across the Atlantic in 1564.

Drake's Secret Logbook
1 June 1564

Here I am at last, heading for where the real action is - the New World!

Tis about time. I am second-in-command of the ship. The captain is not bad, although (guess what?) I reckon yours truly could do a better job!

We captured a few hundred slaves on the African coast. I can't say I enjoyed the work. I'd rather be sailing. Later, as we left Africa behind, we captured some Portuguese slave ships and added their slaves to our own. I know that sounds a bit like piracy, but since the Portuguese stole the slaves in the first place, how can it be?!

We caught the northeast trade winds and sailed for 50 days non-stop, without sight of land in any direction! The fish here have wings and fly out of the water! Gadzooks! What wonders!

Playing Monopoly

Once they had crossed the Atlantic, though, Drake found that trading wasn't as straightforward as it might have been. The problem (as usual) was the pesky King of Spain. Remember how Europe was divided into Catholics and Protestants? Well, the Catholic Pope had issued a Papal Bull (which meant an important bit of paper) saying that the Spanish colonies in the New World (the Americas) could only trade with Spain and Spanish ships – in other words, a monopoly. This Papal Bull went against previous agreements and no one (except Spain) was very happy about it. The Spanish colonies wanted to trade with English ships, but they were not allowed to. The way around it was for everyone to be rather sneaky and do a bit of acting...

How to get round a trade ban (in one easy lesson)
English ship arrives and asks permission to trade.

Later … if asked why he'd allowed the colony to trade with the dreaded English…

WE HAD TO TRADE WITH THEM, THEY HAD GUNS AND EVERYTHING!

The fact that the English ships sold goods much cheaper than the Spanish ships didn't hurt either, of course.

Voyage to misery

Yep, this is the bit where it all goes horribly, horribly wrong. In October 1567, the Hawkins brothers organized another trading expedition and Drake was along for the ride. The fleet consisted of six ships – two of which had been provided by the Queen herself. She probably also invested some royal money in the expedition – Queen Lizzy was always on the look-out for a way to make a bob or two.

The Spanish didn't like the idea of Hawkins sailing across the Atlantic to what they considered their territory. The Spanish Ambassador went to complain to the Queen and to ask where the ships were going. The Queen did what every good, honest head of state would do in those circumstances and lied through her teeth.

Even before they set sail the voyage was troubled. A squadron of seven Spanish men-of-war sailed into Plymouth harbour and had to be chased out with cannon fire.

On 2 October, the expedition set sail for the west coast of Africa in search of slaves. Somewhere along the

African coast they came across a Portuguese caravel that had been abandoned by its crew. The ship was renamed the *Grace of God* – and was given to a brand new captain to command.

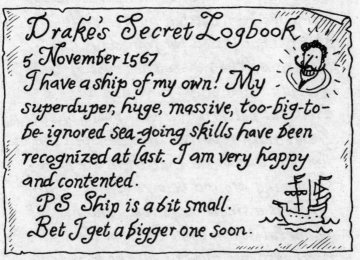

Drake's Secret Logbook
5 November 1567
I have a ship of my own! My superduper, huge, massive, too-big-to-be-ignored sea-going skills have been recognized at last. I am very happy and contented.
PS Ship is a bit small.
Bet I get a bigger one soon.

The crew made slow work of capturing 250 slaves on the coast. As they prepared for the voyage across the mighty Atlantic, Drake was transferred from the small caravel and given the command of the larger *Judith*.

Drake's Secret Logbook
6 February 1568
Told you.

Drake and Hawkins spent several months trading with the Spanish colonies playing 'How to get round a trade ban' each time. Everything was looking good for a swift return to England with their healthy profits when disaster stuck…

Drake's Secret Logbook
15 September 1568

May the merciful saints preserve us! We have been blasted by a terrible storm[1] that lasted for four days and blew us all the way to the coast of Florida. Our ships have had a dreadful battering. The captain of the Jesus hath reported that the splits in her hull are so bad that there are fish swimming around below decks!

After a single day's rest, another powerful storm came in from the northeast and blew us all the way down into the Gulf of Mexico. We are the first English ships ever to sail here.

Now the really BAD news! The only safe harbour of this entire bit of coast is San Juan de Ulua – which is the main Spanish port for the whole of Mexico! One thing's for sure, the Spanish will not be pleased to see us, but what other choice do we have?

[1] Probably the edge of a hurricane – but Drake wouldn't have called it a 'hurricane'.

A bit of a fix

On 16 September, John Hawkins sailed his fleet into the harbour of San Juan de Ulua where, thanks to their faded flags, the locals thought they were the Spanish fleet arriving a bit early.

Taking advantage of the situation, Hawkins quickly seized control. First he sent men to capture the harbour's cannons, then he sent a very polite letter to the governor saying that they had come in peace and that they only wanted time to repair their ships and to buy some supplies.

Everything seemed to be going well, until Hawkins and Drake woke up the next morning (not together) and saw the very unwelcome sight of 13 Spanish ships appearing on the horizon. Onboard one of the warships was a man called Don Martin Enriquez. His name is not important, but his job was – he was the new Viceroy of all the Spanish colonies in South America. Not unreasonably he demanded that he be allowed to enter his own harbour.

Hawkins and Drake were in a fiendishly difficult position. If they wanted, they could use their cannons to keep the Spanish out of their own harbour. The big BIG problem was that doing so would almost certainly be taken as an act of war. If the Spanish didn't kill them, Queen Lizzy was quite likely to chop off their heads when (and if) they got home.

After three days of careful negotiations, Hawkins agreed to let the Spanish ships into the harbour, and in return the Viceroy promised that Hawkins and his men could make their repairs and sail away unharmed.

Things soon got rather crowded:

Everyone got along just fine, until this happened:

THE DAILY DRAKE
23 September 1568

BETRAYED!

Hundreds of English sailors were killed today as they were cruelly betrayed by the sneaky Spanish!

Although they had been promised safe passage, an English fleet of ships belonging to John Hawkins was savagely attacked without warning. It was revealed that the new Spanish Viceroy had secretly ordered hundreds of Spanish soldiers to the port especially to slaughter the English.

A trumpet call gave the signal for the all-out attack to begin. Spanish sailors leapt onboard English ships while Spanish soldiers rushed from their hiding places to overwhelm the English on the shore.

The Spanish greatly outnumbered the exhausted English although our boys fought like tigers against overwhelming odds. The two fleets blasted at each other with their cannons at nearly point-blank range for six hours! Both fleets suffered horrendous damage.

The terrible news for England was that at the end of the brutal battle, FIVE HUNDRED English sailors lay dead! Just two English ships — both badly damaged — managed to escape from the harbour.

THE DAILY DRAKE says: Shame on the Spanish for their cowardly and sneaky attack. It's just not cricket![2]

---

[2] OK, cricket hasn't been invented yet, but you get the idea.

29

Drake's ship, the *Judith*, was first out of the harbour. A combination of difficult weather conditions and thinking that the *Minion* was already lost meant that Drake sailed straight for home.

In fact, John Hawkins was following behind him in the *Minion* on what turned into a nightmare voyage. The ship could barely stay afloat, and the 100 crew members onboard were soon reduced to eating boiled cowhides and the ship's rats (yum!) to survive. By the time the ship limped into Plymouth only John Hawkins and 14 other sailors were left alive. (Drake explained to Hawkins exactly why he'd left, and Hawkins must have forgiven him because the two of them worked together afterwards.)

When the news of the sneaky attack spread across England there was uproar. The already bad relationship between England and Spain was going downhill fast. People demanded revenge.

HOW TO STEAL A MILLION

A lot of people wanted Queen Lizzy to declare war with
Spain. She didn't want to do that, mainly because she
knew England wouldn't win. Spain was simply too
powerful for penniless England to take on in a straight
fight. The Queen's strategy was to wait and build up
England's naval strength, while all the time chipping away
at King Philip's wealth. It was a risky business. Queen
Lizzy and King Philip never actually met after she became
queen, but if they had, it might have looked a bit like this:

At the time, the sneak attack at San Juan De Ulua looked like a huge victory for the Spanish. In the long term, though, the attack had two very VERY important consequences for the Spanish – neither one of which they could possibly have guessed as they celebrated their victory.

The first thing was to do with boat design. After he had recovered from the ordeal of the voyage home, John Hawkins began to look at the design of the English ships. He wanted to work out why some of his ships had been fast enough to get away while other ships had not. With a possible war with Spain looming, a difference in speed of just a few knots could mean the difference between life and death.

POOR HULL SHAPE - SLOWS THE SHIP DOWN BY DRAGGING IN THE WATER

A HIGH FORECASTLE - SLOWS THE SHIP DOWN DUE TO WIND RESISTANCE

* KNOTS - A SHIP'S SPEED WAS MEASURED IN KNOTS. 1 KNOT = 1 NAUTICAL MILE PER HOUR.

Hawkins set about working with the naval dockyards at Woolwich and Deptford, London, on making English ships better. Remember John – we'll met him again in the future when his new designs will prove to be VERY important.

The other consequence of San Juan de Ulua was that the sneaky attack had made Francis Drake very cross indeed. I mean really, really, REALLY cross. Absolutely livid in fact. He had been right in the middle of the fighting and had seen his friends and crew slaughtered before his eyes. It was something that he never forgot and never forgave.

Sailing down the aisle

On 4 July 1569, our boy Drake got married. His blushing bride was called Mary Newman. Other than the fact that she was from Plymouth, we don't know much about Mary. Like most of Drake's life we know far more about what happened to him at sea,  than we do about his life on dry land. The one thing we can be certain of is that Drake didn't spend much time at home. Mary was really Drake's second wife because he was already married ... to the sea.

Back in action

The next year, Drake sailed out of Plymouth harbour in a ship called the *Swan*, heading across the Atlantic. Drake had decided that it was time to take a little revenge on the Spanish. That meant hitting them where it would hurt them most – in their wallets. Drake had already worked out exactly how to do it.

33

Drake decided to sail to the Isthmus of Panama – a place also known as 'that little thin bit in the middle'.

He knew that all the lovely gold and silver that the Spanish were stealing from the Inca people was transported through one small area along the Chagres River. If Drake used a combination of a pinnace to get near the shore and a larger fast ship as his get-away boat then he might be able to swoop in and grab the lot. Crossing the Atlantic once again, Drake wasted no time in putting his plan into action…

Drake's Secret Logbook
March 1571
clever!
Ha! My brilliant plan is working brilliantly. I knew it would. What a goodly genius I am. We used our little pinnace to intercept Spanish merchant ships and then escape close inshore where the big Spanish galleons cannot

sail. So far they have sent three ships after us, but none has come close to capturing us. There is only one master of the sea here and they call him 'Drake'. ⟶

Indeed they did. The Spanish authorities were quick to write to King Philip back in Spain and tell him the bad news…

They are so fully in control of the coast … that traffic dares not sail … and trade and commerce are diminishing…

Drake's Secret Logbook
May 1571
We have stolen the best cargos from over 30 (yes, 30!) ships. By Neptune's beard, 'tis a marvel. One more gold coin and I swear we will sink. We must head home and pray God that we will be received well.

In stealing the Spanish treasure, Drake had acted without the authority of Queen Lizzy. If things had changed at home for the worse, Drake could easily find his head on the block. But when he arrived back, he found that the Queen was only too glad to see him and, of course, the treasure.

The expedition had been such a success that Drake was soon off again. This time he had the smart idea of having three pinnaces made up in kit form and then stored in pieces in the ship's hold. They would be put together when they arrived in South America.

Word spread of Drake's success against the Spanish, and there was soon a queue of people wanting to sail with him aboard his next expedition. Drake chose his crew carefully, knowing that his own life might depend on their skill in a battle or at sea. Drake's brothers John and Joseph also joined the crew.

In May 1572, Drake set sail for the Caribbean once more, with 73 men onboard two ships – the *Swan* and the *Pasco*. Drake was getting used to the route and conditions of the ocean crossing and the voyage took them just 37 days.

Arriving at Port Pheasant, the 'secret' headquarters used during their previous voyage, Drake found a message waiting for him. It had been left by a friendly captain, and basically it said:

Drake decided to stay at Port Pheasant anyway, reasoning that since the Spanish knew he wouldn't go back there because they had discovered its hidden base, then it was the last place that they would actually think of looking for him.

He had the pinnaces put back together, and then started planning a raid on his real target ... the treasure house at a town called Nombre de Dios. This treasure house was where the Spanish stored an entire year's worth of gold and gems stolen from the Incas, as they waited for the Spanish treasure fleet to arrive and take them across the ocean to Spain. Drake had found out the exact layout of the town from Spanish prisoners during his last voyage. He was clever like that.

Drake led the raid on the treasure house himself. Here's what happened. (Warning – it's quite painful.)

Drake's Secret Logbook

29 July 1572

Last night I led a midnight raid of the Nombre de Dios treasure house. A most bold move. I split the men into two groups and we stormed the town from both directions at once. The enemy had time to get off one volley of shots before they fled, and they killed my trumpeter. (Probably the worst review he ever got.)

We reached the treasure house and were preparing to smash open the door when Jer...fainted. Damn and fiddlesticks! I had been shot in the leg with a musketball and hadn't noticed. The men carried me back to the boats at a goodly speed. V.v. embarrassing. Must AVOID getting shot again.

PS Leg still smarts a bit, but God be praised, at least they didn't cut it off.

Drake soon recovered from the musket wound and started planning another raid. He couldn't raid the town again because it would be ready for them. So Drake decided to ambush one of the mule trains that carried the gold to the town. Drake made contact with the *cimarrones* – black slaves who had escaped from their Spanish masters and now lived as free men in the jungle. They knew the jungle well and, in exchange for a share of the treasure, they agreed to help Drake with the ambush.

Time to kill

As they waited for the rainy season to end and the mule trains to start running again, a terrible illness (probably yellow fever) swept through the company, killing 30 of the men in a matter of days.

Disease was a common problem; in fact, dying of a horrible disease was easily the biggest killer of Drake's crewmen on his voyages. Top diseases you were likely to get on a ship included the plague (gives you boils), yellow fever (you go yellow and vomit), gangrene (rotting flesh) and scurvy (caused by lack of vitamins).

Doctors thought most diseases could be cured by using live leeches to suck blood from a patient. They couldn't. Lots of people died.

Drake was desperate to find out what was causing the illness among his men. So desperate that he took the rather gruesome step of asking the ship's doctor to open up one of the bodies to have a look inside. The crew were appalled at the idea, but Drake insisted, and even volunteered the body of his young brother Joseph who had just died.

The ship's doctor opened up the body as requested, but things didn't go very well for him. All he discovered was how to catch the disease himself, and three days later he was dead as well! With good reason, the men called that place Slaughter Island.

The great mule train robbery

As the rainy season ended the mule trains carrying gold and silver started again. Planning to set up an ambush, Drake led a party of his men into the jungle, guided by a group of friendly *cimarrones*. After seven days of battling through thick forest and across dangerous rivers, Drake followed the *cimarrones* as they climbed up steps cut into the side of a very tall tree towards the viewing platform at the top. The sight that waited for him took his breath away.

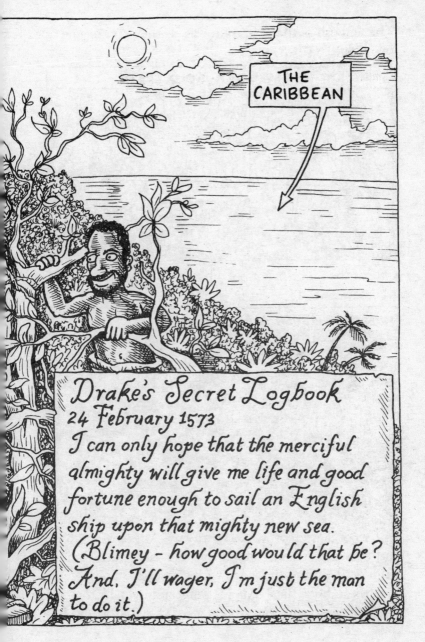

Drake's Secret Logbook
24 February 1573
I can only hope that the merciful almighty will give me life and good fortune enough to sail an English ship upon that mighty new sea.
(Blimey - how good would that be? And, I'll wager, I'm just the man to do it.)

The ambush of the gold train was, as they say, a game of two halves.

One of the sailors leapt out a bit too early and the result was a disaster.

The second attempt worked perfectly. After a very short battle, the 45 guards turned tail and ran away, leaving behind 190 mules all loaded with treasure!

It was a huge haul of gold, gems and over 15 tons of silver. It was valued at around £40,000 (that would be about four million pounds today!). Drake loaded his treasure onboard ship with the rest of his haul and sailed for home with a big (BIG) smile on his face.

Not everyone was happy, of course. The Spanish governors in South America once more wrote to the King of Spain:

> *This realm is at present terrified ... and disturbed.*

It is said that when Drake's ship arrived back in Plymouth a month later it was a Sunday and even respectable people ran from their churches in the middle of a service to see him.

Young Drake was beginning to make something of a name for himself, and the amazing plan he came up with next would write him into the history books for ever.

THE AGE OF DISCOVERY

Our boy Drake was about to be the right man in the right place at exactly the right time to make history. Here's why... And as usual it all comes down to money.

When Drake got back to England and began to tell people his dream of sailing on this new ocean, the Pacific, it fitted in perfectly with the ambitions of the Queen and her advisors. Other countries in Europe, like Spain and Portugal, had been busy sending out explorers and expeditions to lay claim to huge parts of the world, and frankly, little England was being left behind.

Drake's day

Why the world got bigger

In Drake's day the world was a lot smaller. Well, it wasn't really, it was just that people knew a lot less about it. But they were finding out fast, as countries in Europe started sending out explorers all over the place. It was called the Age of Discovery.

This period of exploring had started because traders in Europe had become desperate to find a new route to the Orient (the Far East). Europe loved the smooth silk and the smelly spices that came from the Orient, but the only way the goods could reach Europe was to come all the way over land. As the goods passed through each country, and from trader to trader, everyone added on their own profit so they became more and more expensive.

What the traders in Europe wanted more than anything was a sea route to the Orient so that they could import goods directly and keep all the profit for themselves. In the year 1492, an explorer called Christopher Columbus had set out to sail west across the Atlantic and so find the direct route to China.

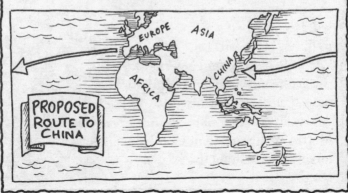

PROPOSED ROUTE TO CHINA

Unfortunately there was one thing stopping him. It was called America.

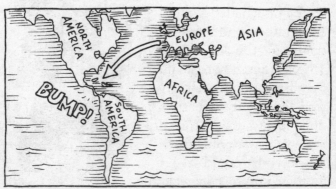

How the world just got bigger and bigger – A brief history

1492 Christopher Columbus sets sail for China but (oops) bumps into America on the way.

1501 Navigator Amerigo Vespucci follows the coast of South America south, still looking for a route to China. (He fails to find one, but does get the entire continent named after him for his efforts after map-maker Martin Waldseemullar forgets that Columbus got there first!)

1513 Vasco Nunez de Balboa walks across the skinny bit where the Americas meet and finds the Pacific Ocean.

AND A LOVELY WALK IT WAS TOO!

1519 Ferdinand Magellan finds a clear route through a narrow strait at the bottom of South America. (A strait is a narrow waterway that connects two large seas.) Magellan becomes the first man to sail around the entire world. (Although he winds up dead before he gets home!)

WHICH IS A SHAME

1519 Spanish adventurer Hernan Cortes discovers and destroys the Aztec civilization of Mexico and steals their gold and silver.

WELL – I'M SURE THEY DIDN'T MIND.

1531 Francisco Pizarro, another Spaniard, slaughters the empire of the Incas and steals their treasure as well.

1570 Slave labour is set to work in the silver mines of Mexico and Peru. The treasure is then shipped back to Spain to pay for armies and ships to conquer any pesky non-Catholic countries like England.

THEY DIDN'T NEED IT!

KA-CHING!

As you can see, all the important discoveries above have one thing in common: NONE of them was made by England. The rest of Europe regarded England as (GASP) pretty second rate when it came to ships and sailing. Queen Elizabeth decided it was time to change all that.

When Lizzy had first come to the throne she had surrounded herself with the brightest brains that England had to offer to advise her. Many of these men were coming to the conclusion that it was time that England started doing a bit of exploring of her own. Two men in particular had convinced the Queen:

Francis Walsingham was the new secretary of state for foreign affairs. He thought that a war with Spain was inevitable and that therefore England should make herself as powerful at sea as she possibly could.

Dr John Dee was one of the sharpest minds in England and was an expert on mathematics, geography, astronomy, as well as astrology. He wrote a book on the idea of founding a 'Brytish Impire.'

By being in the right place at the right time, Drake found that his ambition to sail on the Pacific now exactly matched Queen Lizzy's new ambitions. But where was Drake?

Drake's Secret Logbook
October 1575
What tiresome days. I have spent the last five months in Ireland working for the Earl of Essex. I have been commanding a fleet of small ships ferrying troops around and capturing

rebel shipping.

My tour of duty is now over (praise the Lord!) and I long for voyages further afield. I have a letter from the Earl of Essex recommending me to Sir Francis Walsingham, the new Secretary of State. Perhaps he will have more use for a man of my obvious (and enormous) talents?

Walsingham read the letter and sent for Drake in person. When Drake arrived in his office, Walsingham spread out a map of the world across a table and simply asked Drake:

WHERE DO YOU THINK YOU COULD **MOST** ANNOY THE KING OF SPAIN?

Plans were made for a raiding expedition led by Drake to leave for South America. The investors in the expedition read like a who's who of top posh people. The real plan for the voyage was not written down on paper ANYWHERE for fear that it would fall into the hands of a spy who would alert the Spanish.

Drake soon found himself in a very special meeting.

49

Drake's Secret Logbook
December 1575

Blimey! Today I was commanded to attend a meeting with the Queen herself. I entered the room and before I could even finish my bow, her most eager majesty said, 'Drake! I wish to be revenged upon the King of Spain for the diverse injuries that I have received. You are the only man who might do this exploit.'

I doth find her majesty to be most well informed and a bit of a swot! She asked my advice, and I told her (as I had told Walsingham) that there is little good to be done in attacking him at home in Spain, but that we could annoy him very greatly indeed in the Caribbean and the Pacific.

She then swore me to secrecy and said that anyone who let the king of Spain hear of our plan would lose his head. (Gulp! My lips are sealed.)

me

← me again.

A cunning plan

The plan was for Drake to sail across the Atlantic, then head south along the coast of South America until turning into the dangerous Strait of Magellan and entering the Pacific Ocean. Once in the Pacific Ocean, Drake would be able to 'trade' with the poorly defended Spanish colonies there.

By 'trade', of course, everyone really meant piracy. Queen Lizzy was always on the look-out for ways of making a bob or two and had been more than a bit jealous of the riches that Drake had brought back from his last transatlantic voyage. This expedition had the Queen and several members of her court as investors. They were hoping to upset the king of Spain AND line their own pockets at the same time.

It was vital that the Spanish didn't know where Drake was going, a BIG problem when anything talked about at court might be overheard by Spanish spies. What was needed to protect Drake's secret mission was a cunning plan. In June 1577, ship-owner John Hawkins wrote a letter to Walsingham describing Drake's plans to sail a merchant fleet to North Africa. It was a lot of nonsense, of course, but it wasn't long before the 'information' was reported back by Spanish spies.

Other rumours were spread as well. One said that Drake had been paid a large sum of money to abduct the Prince of Scotland. Before long, the Spanish didn't have a clue where he was headed.

> *It is important for Spain to know the location of their voyage in order to send them to the bottom of the sea.*

To avoid the Spanish finding out where they were really going, Drake decided he wasn't even going to tell the crew until AFTER they had set sail. This also solved another potential problem, which was that if Drake did tell his crew where they were really going then they probably wouldn't go.

The Strait of Magellan (the way into the Pacific via the bottom of South America) had a fearful reputation. It was considered one of the most dangerous and difficult routes to sail in the entire world.

There was a reason that practically no one had repeated Magellan's circumnavigation in the last 55 years. Magellan had spent five weeks battling through appalling weather and terrible storms and had lost two of his ships. (He named it the Pacific Ocean because it meant 'peaceful', which is how it seemed after all the terrible winds in the Strait.) Of the 250 sailors that started the voyage with Magellan, only 18 returned alive, most of them walking skin and bone.

Your mission, should you decide to accept it

Before Drake set off he travelled to London for a farewell meeting with Queen Lizzy. She gave him a green silk scarf on which were embroidered the very cheerful and encouraging words:

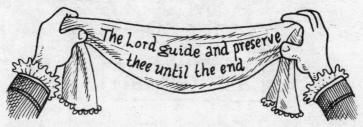

The Lord guide and preserve thee until the end

The incredible journey that Drake was about to attempt would have been extremely difficult and dangerous for an experienced sea captain from Spain or Portugal. For an English captain, sailing into the Pacific Ocean on the opposite side of the world and then coming all the way safely home again must have seemed like Mission Impossible.

Drake rubbed his hands together and couldn't wait to get started.

ALL ABOARD

Drake's fleet was nearly ready to set sail on what would become the longest single sea voyage ever undertaken.

Drake's own ship for the voyage was called the *Pelican*, though later in the voyage she was renamed and is much better remembered as the *Golden Hind*.

FO'C'SLE (FORECASTLE)

THE CREW'S 'TOILET'

GUNDECK- SEVEN CANNONS ON EACH SIDE OF THE SHIP. LOW CEILING SO MEN WORKED ON THEIR KNEES.

THE BRIG

THE PELICAN
NAMED AFTER ONE OF QUEEN LIZZY'S FAVOURITE RELIGIOUS SYMBOLS.

MAINMAST - 30 METRES HIGH

MIZZEN MAST

CAPTAIN'S CABIN

CAPTAIN'S SLEEPING QUARTERS

HOLD - LARGE ENOUGH TO CARRY THE PROVISIONS NEEDED AS WELL AS FOUR PINNACES IN PIECES TO BE ASSEMBLED FOR INSHORE RAIDS.

GREAT CABIN

ARMOURY

GALLERY - OFFICERS' 'TOILET'

BALLAST - HEAVY STONES AT BOTTOM OF HULL TO KEEP THE SHIP STEADY

SIZE - AROUND 120 TONS

Drake had paid for the *Pelican* to be built out of his own pocket. At just over 34 metres long, the *Pelican* was not a particularly big ship, but she had been designed and built to Drake's exact requirements.

The *Pelican* had been built to be Drake's headquarters and floating battle fortress. She could sail in a depth of just 4 metres of water, which meant that she could sail very near the shoreline where many other larger ships would run aground. She had double canvas sails with special bits at the top to increase her speed so she could outrun most other ships.

The *Pelican* carried over 30 tons of cannons and guns, making her a very formidable floating fortress. The fourteen cannons on the gun deck could each blast a metal ball of 4.3 kg, propelling it much further than most other ships' weapons. As if that wasn't enough firepower for one ship, there were also another four cannons mounted on the main deck ready for action.

All the crew had been carefully selected for their different skills. Among them were cooks, carpenters, blacksmiths, a tailor, a shoemaker, several gunners, and of course a ship's surgeon in case anyone needed expert treatment (i.e. their arm or leg cutting off). Drake had also made room for several musicians onboard, partly to entertain the crew and keep them happy, and partly so he could impress whoever he might meet along the way. Drake had the captain's cabin luxuriously furnished and decorated with the same idea in mind i.e. – if it looked a bit flash it might impress the enemy.

Drake's Secret Logbook

15 October 1577

Hath given shopping list to the men.
Hope they can find it all.

KEGS OF TAR

SPARE ANCHOR

SPARE CANVAS

PORTABLE BLACKSMITH'S FORGE

SHIP'S CAT (TO CATCH RATS)

THREE TONS OF GUNPOWDER

AXES, PICKS AND SPADES

BISCUITS

MEAL, DRIED BEEF, CHEESE, BUTTER, RICE, RAISINS, SALT, HONEY AND VINEGAR

PLUS; LANTERNS, TWINE CANDLES, BUCKETS, HOOKS, NEEDLES, CLOTH, SHOES, BEDDING, PLATES, BOWLS, TANKARDS, BRACELETS, LOOKING GLASSES, BEADS, RIBBONS (FOR TRADE), CROSSBOWS, PIKES, LONGBOWS, HELMETS, SWORDS, PISTOLS...

LIVE PIGS

LIVE HENS FOR EGGS

WATER CASKS - ENOUGH FOR ENTIRE CREW FOR SIXTY DAYS

CASKS OF WINE AND BEER

Four other ships joined the *Pelican* to make up the fleet. They were:

The *Elizabeth*: a brand new 80-ton ship provided by the Queen herself.

The *Marigold*: 30 tons in size.

The *Swan*: the provision ship of 50 tons, described as 'flimsy'.

The *Benedict*: a smaller pinnace of 17 tons.

The crew of the fleet numbered 170 men and boys. On the evening of 15 November 1577, Drake's fleet left the harbour at Plymouth to begin its fantastic voyage. However, it was soon back again, and here's why.

Drake's Secret Logbook

18 November 1577

Agggggggggh. Merciful Lord! After months of preparations the fleet finally set sail. We should not have bothered as it was all for naught. With England hardly three hours behind us, the wind turned into a strong gale that then became the worst storm anyone can remember. The only way to stop the *Pelican* and the *Marigold* from capsizing was to cut down their mainmasts! A crying pity. All the ships ended up badly damaged. Rats! 'Tis not the start I was eager for. (Can almost hear the Spanish laughing from here.)

A month later Drake set out again and this time there were no problems. After half a day's sailing, when they were out of sight of land, Drake called the other ships in the fleet alongside the *Pelican* and for the first time told the crew where they were really going – across the Atlantic. This wasn't exactly a big shock for the sailors, some of whom had most likely joined the voyage because they expected Drake to be going on another gold-stealing run to the Caribbean.

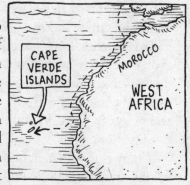

The fleet headed first to Morocco on the coast of North Africa, and then followed the coastline south, heading west to the Cape Verde Islands. On the way, Drake intercepted several little Spanish fishing vessels and put their crews to work providing fish for his own men. This wasn't just an excuse for piracy, though. This was survival. To complete the long voyage across the Atlantic it was vital that Drake restocked their food supplies.

Drake's day

Food

In Drake's day, there were no such things as freezers or tinned food, so making sure you had enough food onboard for a two-month ocean crossing was a real problem. There were 160 mouths to be fed every single day. That's a lot of food.

The basic tactic for long sea voyages was to take as much food as reasonably possible and then stock up again when you had the chance to stop at an island or port. Best of all, steal more food from another ship – especially good if it's a Spanish one!

Fresh fruit and veg would become rotten in the first week of the voyage. Salted meat stored in barrels would last much longer.

CHOMP

One food that never went off was ship's biscuits, a kind of hard-baked biscuit that lasted years even at sea. The only problem was that after a few weeks they would usually be infested with weevils, worms and maggots. (The weevils made a 'crunch' noise as you bit them. Ugh!)

When the ship reached the rich waters of the Caribbean the crew would fish for whatever they could catch. If they went ashore on islands then turtles were easy prey and a ready supply of fresh meat. The ship's cook could keep the poor old turtles alive in some water in the ship's hold until he was ready to make them part of a meal.

Just about any creature that the ship encountered on its travels was likely to end up on the dinner table. Food was cooked on the ship over a fire lit in a large iron firebox that stopped the rest of the ship catching alight.

Perhaps most importantly, from the sailor's point of view, there were also dozens of casks of wine and beer. This wasn't just because the sailors liked a drink (although they certainly did). Onboard ship, normal water quickly became an undrinkable health hazard full of slimy green algae. Beer and wine were a much safer (and more enjoyable) bet.

Local knowledge

As they sailed through the Cape Verde Islands, Drake saw a large Portuguese merchant ship, the *Santa Maria*. Drake gave chase and the speeding *Pelican* quickly captured the craft before it could reach a safe harbour. The *Santa Maria* turned out to have 150 casks of wine and supplies of food in her hold, but she had something even more valuable onboard.

The ship's captain was a man called Nuno de Silva. A quick look at the logbooks in his cabin revealed that he was an experienced sea captain who knew the coast of South America very well. Drake knew the value of someone with local knowledge. He set the rest of de Silva's crew free, and took the Portuguese captain with him to act as his guide. It was a smart move.

CONGRATULATIONS, YOU'VE JUST WON A FREE HOLIDAY

Across the Atlantic

Although Drake had done it before, sailing across the Atlantic Ocean was still a big, BIG deal. The fleet would be out of sight of land for weeks and weeks. It was vitally important that it stayed together and that discipline was maintained on all the ships. If one of the crew had kept a scrapbook during the crossing it might have looked something like this.

me and the captain. I think he likes me.

Passed erupting volcano on Fogo in the Cape Verde islands. Volcano blasted ash and smoke six miles into the air.

plague of lice drop in for a bite (of us).

After 63 days at sea, the fleet finally sighted the coast of Brazil, and, boy, were they happy to see dry land.

Land of the demons

With Drake in the *Pelican* leading the way, the fleet sailed straight into a thick fog that had suddenly appeared from inshore. As they headed towards the coast, the sailors measuring the depth of the water (with a line) were suddenly alarmed and alerted Drake. Da Silva urged him to turn round quickly – the shoals (or shallows) extended far further from the coast than was normal. The fleet turned away just in time, with one ship's hull scraping along the bottom. The fleet had been just moments from total disaster. Drake's decision to bring Da Silva with them had saved their lives.

Instead of going ashore, Drake decided to head south along the coast. As they continued slowly through the dense fog, da Silva told Drake and his men that this area of coast was known to the Portuguese as 'Terra Demonum' or Land of the Demons. The Portuguese believed this was an area ruled by Indians who had sold their souls to the devil in exchange for strange powers, including the ability to create terrible storms and blinding fog. Gulp!

In a world where most people still believed in witchcraft and the supernatural, these stories must have terrified Drake's sailors who were already further from home than any English ship had ever been. Things got worse when, within the hour, a violent gale blew in from the south and split up the fleet.

When the storm finally subsided, Drake kept the *Pelican* heading south and found his missing ships at a pre-arranged meeting point. Drake was so pleased he named the place Cape Joy. Over the next few weeks they sailed hundreds of miles along the coast, always heading south. The crew went ashore to gather fresh water and food supplies whenever they could. On one expedition the men found an island of sea lions – so no guesses what they had for dinner that night. (It's a good life, being a sailor.)

It was now May 1578 and Drake's fleet had been at sea for six months. They had successfully navigated across the Atlantic and now sailed further south along the coast of South America than any English ship had ever been before. The fleet was alone, thousands and thousands of miles from home, and sailing along an unknown and hostile coastline.

ISLAND OF BLOOD

The next leg of Drake's voyage was full of arguments, bloodshed and grisly deaths. The fleet continued to sail its way southwards along the coast of South America, heading to a place called Port San Julian.

It was the middle of June, which is mid-winter in the southern hemisphere where the seasons are the upside-down-twisty-turny reverse of the north.

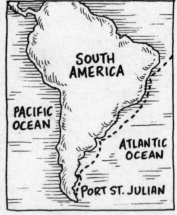

As the brave boys of the fleet sailed south the temperature dropped and the weather was getting worse. Drake knew that he would have to wait until spring (October) before he could attempt to sail through the Strait of Magellan to his ultimate goal – the Pacific Ocean. Drake must have suspected that there were difficult times ahead.

Drake's Secret Logbook
16 June 1578

Perhaps 'twas a mistake to have kept our destination quite so secret. Thirty crewmen are still angry because they were expecting a six-month trip to the warm Caribbean and instead I have sailed them to the cold, frozen end of the earth. The men are fearful of the dreaded Strait of Magellan that lies ahead. I don't blame them – they rightly reckon it as the most perilous part of our voyage. Must watch for any talk of mutiny.

shiver shiver

Port San Julian was the location that Ferdinand Magellan himself had used as his headquarters although, his stay had not been a happy one – a fact that Drake's entire crew knew only too well. This was the place where Magellan's officers had attempted a mutinous takeover of his ship. One of the officers was hanged and two were left marooned.

The reputation of the place was spooking out Drake's men before they even got there. What they needed was a nice quiet afternoon ashore, a bit of a walk in the sun, and certainly no sudden death and bloodshed. Fat chance. Drake led a landing party on to shore and here's what happened...

Drake and his men were attacked by several dozen Indians with bows and arrows. The master gunner was killed and the ship's doctor was badly injured (and died two days later). Only quick thinking by Drake saved their lives when he grabbed a gun dropped by one of his men. Drake fired it at the nearest Indian, things got VERY messy and the rest ran off.

This wasn't the welcome they'd been hoping for but despite their bad beginning, Drake decided to stay in Port San Julian. Perhaps he simply didn't want to spend time and energy looking for a new headquarters along the coast.

Drake was planning to spend the next two months gradually refitting and repairing his battered fleet as well as allowing his men to get some rest. There was, however, a much more difficult and urgent problem for Drake to deal with and his name was Thomas Doughty.

The trouble with Thomas

Thomas Doughty first met Drake when they were serving in Ireland together. Doughty was about the same age as

Drake, but he was a gentleman – which meant that his family had lots of money and he was really posh. (Drake, remember, wasn't.)

Thomas Doughty was also clever, well educated, and very very ambitious. He and Drake had quickly become firm friends, and Drake probably recommended him to be one of the gentlemen on this voyage. (The crew was divided into posh gentlemen who often sat around and did no work, and the common sailors who hardly ever sat around and who did ALL the work.)

During the voyage, however, the relationship between Drake and Doughty had really hit the rocks. Doughty liked to swan around doing absolutely nothing, which made him very unpopular with the working sailors (but quite popular with the other gentlemen). Before they'd even left England, he had claimed to one of the crew that he shared command with Drake. He didn't.

Things started getting messy when some of the sailors accused Doughty of stealing from one of the ships they'd captured. To make things even more of a mess, Doughty had been quietly asking around to see if anyone fancied a bit of mutiny.

Drake wasn't happy. He wasn't happy at all. In fact the two had a VERY heated argument, after which Drake had Doughty tied to the ship's mast for two days. Doughty's trouble-making talk was in danger of spreading to others in the crew just as Drake needed them all to pull together. Drake had a serious dilemma.

Drake's Secret Logbook

25 June

Gadzooks, 'tis tough being a brilliant commander these days. Even my mighty captain's brain is tired out with the problem of what to do about Thomas Doughty?

My options -

1 Do nothing - which risks him leading a mutiny and me getting it in the neck.

me →

2 Charge Doughty with mutiny and have his head chopped off - which risks him causing a mutiny and me getting it in the neck.

me again

I must take my time and give due consideration to all arguments.

PS Have decided. I didn't get where I am today (the end of the world) by doing nothing. If anyone's head is coming off, 'tis Doughty's, not mine.

PPS I will arrange a fair and neutral trial so he can be found guilty ASAP.

70

On 30 June, Drake got the entire ship's company together and charged Thomas Doughty with mutiny. Doughty said he was innocent very loudly indeed.

Drake had a rather large jury of 40 of the crew sworn in for Doughty's trial. Both sides called witnesses, but it was Doughty himself who was responsible for his own downfall. While being questioned by Drake, Doughty admitted that he had given away details of their top-secret mission before they had set sail. Without realizing it, Doughty had admitted that he had broken the strict orders of secrecy given by the Queen. If he wasn't in trouble before then, he certainly was now.

The jury returned a verdict of guilty. Drake wanted to execute Doughty, rather than have him hang around to cause more unrest among the crew, and two days later the 'Island of Blood' claimed its victim. The executioner's axe removed Doughty's head with a single blow, and then it was held up as a warning for the rest of the crew.

WHERE NO (ENGLISH) MAN HAS GONE BEFORE

With the troublesome Doughty now headless, Drake turned his attention to making some much-needed repairs to his fleet. If the ships were not kept in the best possible state then the expedition could easily be sunk.

Before the fleet could sail on, all the ships needed to be thoroughly 'careened'. When wooden ships were at sea for long periods their hulls gradually got covered in barnacles and seaweed. A ship that had been at sea for months could be dragging a very heavy mass of seaweed through the ocean with it, which would really slow it down. Careening meant that the ships were emptied completely and then gently run aground on to a beach. The crew cleaned first one side of her hull and then the other, before finally painting the hull with hot tar. After her sails were repaired, she was refloated and was shipshape once more.

Careening had to be done, but Drake soon had more than just that to worry about…

Drake's Secret Logbook
3 August 1578

By the merciful heavens, we must get moving! 'Tis time we were leaving this 'Island of Blood'. With the ships being careened, the entire company is sleeping ashore in tents. The night often brings snow and the men awake with a tiresome damp chill in their bones. Food is becoming a grave problem as there is little to hunt here and we have come to exist on ship's biscuits. (Ugh!) 'Tis not yet the end of winter, but we must be away from here with a goodly haste.

yuk!

The diet was soon so bad that some of the men started to suffer from scurvy (caused by a lack of the vitamins found in fresh fruit and vegetables). Sailors with scurvy found that their gums slowly went rotten and their teeth began to fall out. Bad cases could lead to painful boils on the body and eventually even death.

Drake was well ahead of his time in preventing scurvy among his crews. He didn't know about vitamins, but the canny sea captain had worked out that it was a good idea to add fresh fruit and fish to the men's diet whenever he could. The crewmen that got the most sick were given a soup made of mussels and seaweed, which at least stopped them getting any worse.

But Drake faced several problems. There was the continuing bitter cold, the sickness among the crew, and the fearful prospect of having to navigate the Magellan Strait. However, none of these concerned Drake as much as the fact that (despite Doughty no longer being around to stir up trouble) the sailors and the gentlemen were still not getting along. Drake knew that if the crew did not work together they were doomed.

The ships were finally ready to sail on 11 August, and Drake called the entire crew together so he could speak to them. With the his men assembled on the beach in front of him, Drake made the most important speech of his life. It went something like this...

My masters, I am a very bad speaker, for my bringing up hath not been in learning, but what I shall say let all men take good notice of.

We are very far from our country and our friends. We are surrounded on every side by our enemies. We cannot afford to lose a single man for we could not replace him even if we would give ten thousand pounds for one. Yet there is such trouble between the sailors and the gentlemen that it does make me mad just to hear of it.

From this moment on I must have the gentleman hauling and drawing with the mariner, and the mariner with the gentleman. We must show ourselves as a company. Let us not give occasion to the enemy to rejoice at our decay. I would know him that would refuse to set his hand to a rope, but I know that there is not any such here.

It was practically unheard of for a commander to ask the la-de-da gentlemen to get off their backsides and actually work. Drake said that anyone who didn't like his new rules could lump it, and offered to spare the *Marigold* to ship home any man who wished to go. The reports of the voyage all record that the entire crew was agreed that they wanted to sail on under Drake's terms.

He then asked the men if they would rather have regular wages, OR if they would 'stand to his courtesy', which meant that the crew would share in whatever treasure they brought home. Again the response was unanimous.

Drake had one more trick up his sleeve when he surprised everyone by calling forward all his officers and relieving them of their commands. There was much wailing and gnashing of teeth from the sacked officers. Drake then reappointed nearly all of them, making it clear to them who had given them their jobs and making it crystal clear exactly who was in charge of the fleet.

Drake then ordered his men back on to their ships, and gave the order for the fleet to set sail south towards the unknown terrors of Magellan's Strait.

Enter the *Golden Hind*

Before they attempted the dangerous strait, Drake had one more loose end to tie up. Drake was worried that when they got back to England and top posh bloke Sir Christopher Hatton heard that Drake had executed his chum (Thomas Doughty) then Hatton might not be too happy. Drake knew that posh people love a bit of flattery and he also knew that Hatton's family crest featured a female deer known as a 'hind'.

On the morning they approached Magellan's Strait, Drake held a renaming ceremony and changed the name of the *Pelican* to the *Golden Hind*. It was a calculated piece of grovelling designed to get him off the hook back in England. That is, of course, assuming that they got back to England.

The Magellan Strait

It is difficult to imagine how Drake and his crew must have felt as they prepared to enter the dreaded Magellan Strait. They were thousands of miles from home, with absolutely no hope of rescue if things went wrong. No Englishmen before them had ever dared to try and sail through the Strait.

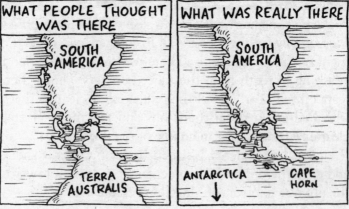

As far as the English were concerned, this was the end of the known world and Drake was just about to sail right over the edge. Here's how he might have described it.

Drake's Secret Logbook

20 August

Ye gads! We are finally into this devil of a strait. White sea spray beats on to the dark cliffs here as if eager to send them crashing down. The tides here are unnaturally powerful and the ocean floor is littered with sharp rocks. Pray God. We will need double our wits to survive this.

21 August

Conditions are getting worse. Violent storms tumble down the steep mountain slopes, churning up the ocean in front of us. ('Tis a worry that one will hit us directly!)

22 August

Forty miles into the strait and the wind is still increasing. As our goodly fleet sailed past, the Indians lit huge fires on the shore - an eerie sight in this strange land.

24 August

Anchor near three islands and claim them for our own dear England. Land on the largest and name it Elizabeth Island after our most glorious (and far away) queen. Cut down a bit of tree to take home to Lizzy. She'll like that. (I hope.)

The islands are teeming with strange black-and-white birds that the sailors are calling 'pen gwinns'. I'll wager there are thousands of them on a single island, and the birds swim instead of fly. No need to ask what's for dinner tonight.

25 August

Dinner was delicious. Ordered men to slaughter 3,000 more 'pen gwinns' to keep us going for a bit. Yum. After dark, an erupting volcano to the south lit up the night sky with an unnatural red glow. We are truly at the edge of the world.

The conditions in the strait meant that nothing was easy. For a start, Drake found that although there were plenty of good harbours, the water was so deep that it was practically impossible to find a place to anchor.

Next there were the winds. The strait was bordered on both sides by high, snow-topped mountains whose peaks were hidden in the clouds. Unpredictable gusts of wind would suddenly come whirling down from the mountaintops and the men had to work hard just to avoid being blasted on to the rocks of the opposite shore.

A one point it looked as if the strait reached a dead end and Drake took a small boat ahead of the *Golden Hind* to ensure that there was a way through. There was, and in September 1578 the two English ships left Magellan's Strait behind them and sailed out into the Pacific Ocean.

To mark the fleet's passage through the strait in one piece, Drake had a metal plaque engraved. He intended to set up a little monument to their marvellous achievement on Cape Deseado (the pointy bit at the end of the strait). When the wind strengthened during the day, the plan had to be abandoned or they would have risked being smashed to pieces on the rocks. (A bit of a high price to pay for putting up a plaque to yourself.)

Plaque or no plaque, they were through the dreaded Magellan's Strait. Drake had done it.

STORMY WEATHER

The only map that Drake had of where they were now was extremely dodgy. Drake headed northwest, expecting to follow the coastline, but soon found himself on the open seas in the middle of a powerful storm. The monstrous waves dwarfed their ship.

The storms were so violent that the sails had to be removed from the masts to stop them from snapping. Storm after storm battered them for three long weeks, pushing them further and further in a southwest direction.

Amazingly the three ships of the fleet managed to remain within sight of each other. That is until the morning of 28 September when the men reported to Drake that the *Marigold* had vanished. One of the crew on night watch claimed to have heard the cries of men in the night.

And then there was one

While they were attempting to come to anchor one night, Drake's remaining ships, the *Golden Hind* and the *Elizabeth* became separated. Drake had already set a meeting place north on the coast of Chile in case the ships lost each other. But Captain John Winter, in charge of the *Elizabeth*, had other ideas. Realizing that Drake was nowhere in sight, he ordered the *Elizabeth* to head back into Magellan's Strait – the exact opposite direction from the agreed meeting point. Captain Winter then spent a little time 'looking' for Drake, though his idea of looking went something like this.

I CAN'T SEE HIM, I CAN'T SEE HIM.

After they had had a little rest, an exhausted and stressed Captain Winter ordered his crew to turn around and head back for England. His decision to desert Drake was against the wishes of many of his crew who wanted to stay and get rich.

Putting the maps right

Even as the *Elizabeth*'s crew was obeying captain's orders and heading home, Drake was searching for *them*. It was hard going because the poor old *Golden Hind* once more found herself blown hundreds of miles to the south by gales. Still, one good thing did come out of it. Remember, at the time of Drake's voyage, people thought that the Magellan Strait was the only sailable route between the Atlantic and the Pacific Oceans. They thought that the land to the south of the strait was the beginning of some massive supercontinent that spread as far as the South Pole.

Blown there by one storm after another, Drake could now see that there was no great continent sitting there. Only the great rolling ocean where the Atlantic meets the Pacific.

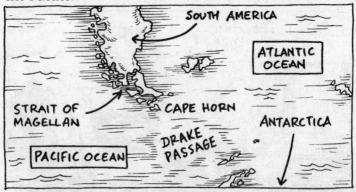

No one knows exactly how far south Drake got, but the passage there was named after him in honour of the fact that he was probably the first man ever to see it.

Pretty as a picture

When Drake set sail for the coast of South America, the Queen and her advisors knew that if things went well then he would be the first Englishman to see many sights. The Queen gave Drake strict instructions that he was to keep a full and complete record of his journey AND to map and record the coastlines that he found. Any information that Drake could bring back about the locations of safe harbours, dangerous sandbanks, and sources of fresh water and food would be invaluable to future English sea captains following after him.

Drake took the responsibility very seriously. He knew (or rather hoped) that he was writing himself into the history books and wanted to be remembered for the discoveries that he was making.

Keeping a journal (or log, as a sea captain would call it) meant lots of writing by longhand. According to Nuno da Silva, the captured pilot:

> *Drake carries a book in which he writes his log of the voyage and paints birds, trees, and seals. He is diligent in painting and carries along a relative, a boy called John Drake who is a great painter. When they both shut themselves up in his cabin, they were always painting.*

83

Because there were no digital cameras or any way of taking photographs in Drake's day, the only way of recording what they saw was to draw or paint it. Drake was determined to record the coast as accurately as he could.

Drake's paintings of the coast got the Spanish really worried. Don Francisco de Zarate, one of Drake's many prisoners, was so alarmed he wrote:

He also carries painters who paint for him pictures of the coast in its exact colours. This I was most grieved to see, for each thing is so naturally depicted that no one who guides himself with them could go astray.

Lost

When he returned, Drake's journals and charts from this amazing voyage were considered so important that they were all turned over to the Queen and subject to an oath of secrecy. They were hidden somewhere safe, somewhere so safe that pretty soon they were lost. Some people think that they were destroyed when London's Palace of Whitehall burned down in 1698, while other people think that they might still be hidden somewhere in one of England's old buildings. (They'd be worth millions today, so if you've got any ideas where they might be, let us know!)

All alone in the world

Although Drake didn't know it yet, he was now all alone. The *Marigold* had indeed sunk with the loss of all its crew, and even as Drake searched for it, the *Elizabeth* was threading her way back through Magellan's Strait towards home. Drake was now left with one ship, and a crew of just 80 or so men and boys. Anyone else might have thought twice about continuing on their mission to plunder from the King of Spain, but not our Drake.

Having been battered by storms for practically the entire two months since emerging from Magellan's Strait, Drake finally found good sailing weather. He headed north along the coast of South America towards the agreed meeting point at the latitude of 30° off the coast of Chile. They made good speed, covering over 1,200 miles in just a few weeks. It was the middle of summer in the southern hemisphere, and the days were hot and long.

On 25 November, the *Golden Hind* came to anchor at the island of Mocha, and Drake led a heavily armed landing party ashore. The party encountered some Indians, and Drake traded with them for some food. They seemed friendly enough and Drake left them saying that the next day he would come back again to get supplies of fresh water.

When Drake and his men returned the following morning, they were ambushed by more than 100 Indians who unleashed a ferocious hail of arrows at them. Drake was hit just under his right eye and on his head, the master gunner was killed, and the rest of the men were hit with anything between five and twenty arrows each. Drake and Co made a quick escape…

Drake's Secret Logbook
26 November 1578

The men want to revenge themselves upon the Indians with cannon shot, but I have forbidden them to do so. I reason that the Indians had mistaken us for Spaniards who have killed and enslaved more than enough Indians to warrant the treatment that we accidentally received in their place. We shall sail on with no thoughts of vengeance.

Pirates of the Pacific

After continuing up the coast for about a week, Drake reached the port of Valparaiso where he saw just a single ship, the *Capitana*, in the harbour. The crew of the *Capitana* thought that only Spanish ships sailed in the Pacific, so seeing the *Golden Hind* slowly approaching the crew got out their best drum to give the new ship a proper welcome. It wasn't until Drake's boarding party was actually on her deck that the *Capitana*'s crew realized their mistake.

In her hold were 75 pounds of gold (well worth the effort then!) and nearly 2,000 jars of wine. (Drake's crew enjoyed a little drink that evening.) Rather than empty her hold, Drake decided to steal the whole ship. He put 25 of his crew aboard and the next day she set sail with the *Golden Hind*.

They sailed north and were soon at 30° latitude, the appointed rendezvous point with Drake's two missing ships, the *Marigold* and the *Elizabeth*. Drake criss-crossed the ocean for five days before finally accepting he would not see either of them again.

Merry Christmas, Captain Drake

During a trip ashore to get water, the landing party came under surprise attack by a squad of Spanish horsemen accompanied by 200 Indians on foot. One of the sailors,

Richard Minivy, was killed. As an expression of how welcome English sailors were, the Spanish soldiers took his still-warm corpse and chopped off his head, cut out his heart and then let the Indians use what was left for target practice.

Drake sailed north once more and the next day he found what he was looking for – a safe bay to careen and repair the ships. The *Golden Hind* was especially in need of attention after all those storms she'd had to cope with.

Knowing how to handle his men was one of Drake's great skills, and he knew that after what they'd been through, most of the men needed rest. The week of Christmas was declared by Drake to be a time of rest and on New Year's Day 1579, Drake sat down with his entire crew for 'a giant feast' in honour of the New Year.

The careening operation took the usual three weeks and by 19 January 1579 Drake's two ships, the *Golden Hind* and the captured *Capitana*, were underway once more. During a raid ashore in the harbour of Africa (a bit of a confusing name for a port in South America), Drake heard that a treasure ship containing over 1,300 bars of gold and silver had left the port only two days before, heading north to Chule, the next port. Drake gave chase in the *Golden Hind*, straining every sail in an effort to catch up with the Spanish treasure ship.

When they reached Chule, Drake saw the ship in the harbour and swooped towards it. As he got nearer he saw that it was wet above the waterline all around its hull – a sure sign that it had just been emptied of its cargo. Drake had missed out. A messenger on horseback had been sent from Africa to warn the town of Drake's presence.

This was very bad news indeed for our favourite pirate, sorry, sea captain. Drake had few men at his command, and was surrounded by enemies, but the one thing he did have on his side was the element of surprise. If all the Spanish ports knew he was coming then his treasure-seeking mission would be much, MUCH harder.

All was not lost, but Drake knew he had to act quickly. Experience told him that all he really needed for successful treasure raids was one fast ship (the *Golden Hind*) and a smaller pinnace or two. With this in mind, he ordered his crew to abandon the three vessels that they had captured along the way. The men set up the sails and sent them out to sea as deserted ghost ships.

Drake also knew that the *Golden Hind* could sail quicker than a rider could ride over land. Drake left the harbour of Chule behind him, and ordered his men to sail north as fast as they could. The *Golden Hind* covered nearly 500 miles in a mad five-day dash. Would even that be enough to outrun news of their presence?

THE DRAGON

Drake's first target was the port of Callao, the main port of Peru and Chile. The amount of gold and silver that passed through it in a year was enough to buy a small country. Drake also knew that both the port and its ships were poorly defended. It's hard not to imagine him rubbing his hands together at the prospect.

A little way south of Callao, the *Golden Hind* spotted a small trading ship and quickly captured her. The captain didn't take much persuading to spill the beans about ship movements in the area.

Midnight raid

Drake never underestimated the usefulness of local knowledge. He used what the captain had told him to plan a daring raid on the port. Under cover of night, the *Golden Hind* sailed right into the harbour. There were 17 ships at anchor, all of them empty of men and treasure except for one chest of silver coins. Drake wasn't pleased. Just as things weren't going well anyway, they suddenly got a whole lot worse. As the harbourmaster was rowing out to greet the *San Cristobel*, a new arrival, he spotted the cannons of the *Golden Hind* outlined against the starry sky.

The harbourmaster gave the alarm and soon the port was in uproar. The only thing Drake could steal was the *San Cristobel* itself. Its crew put up a fight until Drake sent a cannon-ball blasting through one side of the ship and out the other! The fight didn't last long after that, and Drake made his escape into the night.

When dawn broke the next day, a Spanish general loaded two ships full of troops and gave chase to Drake who was now becalmed a way outside the harbour. Drake had his men prepare for a fight, but the general had made a bad mistake and had not had the ships ballasted. (Ballast was heavy things that went in the ship's hold to keep her steady at sea.) As a result, the ships rolled so badly that everyone onboard was very, very ill indeed.

Drake made his get-away while the ships limped back into harbour feeling very sorry for themselves.

The big prize

Raiding the port of Callao had turned out to be a bit of a damp squib, but Drake had learned that a huge Spanish treasure galleon, the *Cacafuego* had recently set sail. She was loaded with silver, and the fact that it belonged personally to King Philip of Spain was a delightful bonus for Drake. The *Cacafuego* had a ten-day start over Drake's ship, but was scheduled to call at a few ports along the way. Drake ordered his crew to give chase.

As they got closer, Drake offered a reward of a gold chain to the first person to spot the treasure galleon.

As they crossed the equator, John Drake (Drake's brother) gave a cry from the crow's nest. The *Cacafuego* was on the horizon. Here's what happened next…

Drake's Secret Logbook

1 March 1579

I am a genius – even if I do say so myself. (And I do!) After we spied the *Cacafuego*, I was worried that her crew might spot that we were an English ship. So I had the men put strings of wine jars full of water trailing behind us in the sea. (How brilliant is that?!) With all our sails left up, but the wine jars slowing us down, we looked like a merchant vessel heavy with cargo instead of a swift English fighting ship captained by a handsome sea-going legend such as myself. My trick worked a treat. Once we got close, one of our heavy guns blew their mizzenmast into the sea and they couldn't surrender quickly enough.

PS My crew are lucky to have such a great captain telling them what to do. Must remember to lower their wages.

What we got:

1,300 bars of silver (weight 26 tons!)

13 chests stuffed with silver coins

80 pounds of gold

There was so much treasure that it took Drake's crew three whole days to move it from ship to ship, replacing the ballast stones in the *Golden Hind*'s hold with gold and silver. (They also helped themselves to food and some of the Spanish ship's fittings as well.)

Drake explained to the captain of the ship, San Juan de Anton, why he was taking the treasure. It was compensation, he said, for the English lives lost when the sneaky Spanish betrayed the English at San Juan de Ulua. (Remember that nasty night? – See page 28.) Was this just an excuse or did Drake really believe the English were owed compensation? Probably a bit of both. Drake also told the Spanish captain that if the King of Spain did not begin to allow English ships to trade legally with his colonies then Drake would return to claim yet more silver.

Drake was developing something of a reputation for being exceptionally nice to his prisoners. During Captain Anton's three-day stint as a captive aboard Drake's ship he had eaten all his meals at Drake's own table and he'd been (like the rest of his crew) treated very well.

Trickster

Drake knew that after capturing such a big prize as the treasure ship news of the event would travel everywhere. The Spanish were bound to send ships after him now – they had to as a matter of pride. Drake decided to create a diversion to keep the Spanish from chasing him. As he prepared to set free the crew of the (now empty) treasure ship he gave many of them little gifts of money or goods. To Captain Anton, Drake gave a letter he had written personally. It was a letter of safe conduct and it went something like this…

Dear Captain Winter [3]
If you should meet with Captain Anton, then I ask that you treat him well. If you take any supplies from his ship then please pay him well for them. You should order that none of your soldiers do him harm or injury.

This letter is not just for Captain Winter, but also for all the other English captains in our mighty fleet: Captain Thomas, Captain Arle, Captain Tombe, Captain Anthony and the rest of our friends.
Amen,
Francis Drake

[3] Captain of the now-on-it's-way-home *Elizabeth*.

95

Drake knew that as soon as he set his captives free the letter would be sent to the Spanish authorities. If Spanish ships and ports were expecting more attacks from a large English fleet then they would have less time to chase him. Much less time. Drake's cunning ploy worked. The thought of more English ships loose in the Pacific was enough to make even the bravest Spanish general shake a bit. Several Spanish ships were sent southwards looking for the rest of Drake's non-existent fleet.

When the all the treasure had finally been transferred, Drake was as good as his word and set his captives free aboard their own ship. Then with the biggest treasure trove of his entire career safely in the *Golden Hind*'s hold, Drake set a course heading north and disappeared into the warm tropical night.

Horribly famous

Over the following months, news of Drake's success began to leak back to Europe. The news was greeted rather differently in the courts of Spain and England.

In England, Drake's backers were reported as being '*beside themselves with joy*' when they heard the news. Not everyone in England was quite as happy, though. London merchants were terrified that the King of Spain would seize their property and ships in revenge for the stuff Drake had stolen. The Queen told her council to assure them that Drake was on a strictly private voyage, and that King Philip could not hold England responsible for his actions. (Of course, that was a huge fib.)

Spanish officials in South America had to write letters to the King of Spain explaining just how come Drake had been so successful at stealing all the King's money. It wouldn't have been a good idea for them to admit how unprepared and useless their defences were, so they pretended that Drake was even more scary and smart than he already was. As Drake's reputation grew his enemies came to believe all sorts of things about him...

• That he had a magic mirror. It was supposed to be kept in secret in his cabin and let him look over the horizon to spot ships that other captain couldn't see.

• That he controlled the weather and could summon rain or wind as he wished.

• That he was the Devil in human form.

Well, if you're getting beaten by someone with superpowers then you don't need to feel so bad about losing, do you?

Carry on sailor

After the success with the treasure, Drake continued to sail north. The *Golden Hind* was both weighted down with treasure and also in desperate need of another careening session. Although the ship was moving more slowly than she should, Drake knew he couldn't stop now. He had to concentrate on putting as much distance between him and any pursuers as possible.

The *Golden Hind* covered 600 miles in nine days to reach the coast of Costa Rica. The crew made the usual search for fresh water and food. While they were enjoying their dinner of monkey and alligator, a massive earthquake shook the ship that *'did shake and quiver as if it had been on dry land.'*

A few days later they captured a merchant ship. One of its passengers was a posh nobleman called Don Francisco de Zarate and he described Drake like this:

> *He is called Francisco Drac, and is a man about 35 years of age, low of stature with a fair beard, and is one of the greatest mariners that sails the seas, both as a navigator and as a commander.*

It was now March 1579. We know that by November 1579, Drake had sailed the *Golden Hind* to the Philippines, but what he did and exactly where he went over the next eight months are one of the great mysteries of the Elizabethan age…

THE DRAKE MYSTERY

Exactly what our daring sea captain Drake did next is the biggest mystery of his entire round-the-world voyage. The question that has caused several punch-ups between historians over the years is: How far north did Drake explore along the west coast of North America?

CALIFORNIA! CANADA! ALASKA!

The one thing that (nearly) everyone does agree on is that Drake got at least far as California. So where in California did he land? Er ... well, nobody can agree.

Location location location

After Drake returned to England, many details of the voyage were kept secret for ever, and those maps that were released had the latitudes of places changed. This was done to make it much harder (near impossible) for the Spanish and others to use maps of the later bit of Drake's voyage. The big problem is that because all the original papers have since been lost it also makes it hard (or nearly impossible) for us to work out exactly where he went.

It's generally accepted that Drake probably landed somewhere around the San Francisco bay area. People who live in the area today certainly like to think that he did. On the coast there's a Drake's Bay and in town you can book yourself into the posh Drake's Hotel or attend the Drake High School.

Remember that engraved plate that our hero was going to set up to mark them coming through the Strait of Magellan, but then couldn't because of a storm? (See page 79) Well in 1936, someone claimed to have found just such a brass plate near San Francisco.

When it was first found everyone thought it was genuine and got very excited, then everyone said it was a hoax. Years later they decided it was genuine again, then years after that they decided it was a hoax again.

The plate is kept in the library at the University of California if you want to have a look and decide for yourself.

Did Drake go further north?

A few people think that Drake might have got further north. A lot further north.

It's been suggested that as a secret part of his mission from the Queen, Drake was looking for two things. Firstly, a good location to found an English colony far from prying Spanish eyes in South America. Secondly, that Drake may have been searching for the legendary Strait of Anian.

Drake's day

In Drake's day, people wanted to find a get-rich-quick route to the spice-rich islands of the Pacific. Getting there meant sailing around either the bottom of Africa (the Cape of Good Hope) or the bottom of South America (via the Strait of Magellan).

The clever people who drew maps decided that there must be a clear sailing route over the top of North America, linking the North Atlantic and the Pacific. They called this the Strait of Anian.

102

Why did they think the Strait of Anian existed? Well, basically because they wanted it to, and it would have been jolly convenient. It didn't exist; the frozen North Pole was in the way for a start.

It's been suggested that finding (and following) the Strait of Anian was possibly one of the main objectives of the voyage. If it *had* existed, and if England had found it before Spain, then it would have given queen Lizzy an enormous boast in her cold war with King Philip.

So did Drake really go north?

There is some evidence that suggests he did… Some maps drawn after Drake's voyage show accurate features on the northwest coastline of America. Drake's record of the voyage was lost but other records mention that they sailed so far north that the crew complained about the bitter cold…

The very ropes of our ship were stiff and the rain which fell was an unnatural congealed and frozen substance, so that we seemed rather to be in the frozen zone.

Drake's men were moaning about the cold so much that he named that area the Coast of Objections.

Another plate

One fascinating piece of evidence may have been found by a man called Donald McDonald (yep, that's his real name). Here's what happened…

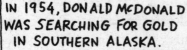

IN 1954, DONALD McDONALD WAS *SEARCHING FOR GOLD* IN SOUTHERN ALASKA.

HE DECIDED TO EXPLORE A CAVE ON THE MOUNTAINSIDE.

THE CAVE CONTAINED SOME BURIED INDIAN BONES AND A SMALL PIECE OF METAL PLATE.

HE TOOK THE PLATE HOME AND CLEANED IT. IT HAD SOME ODD WRITING ON IT THAT HE DIDN'T RECOGNIZE.

HE TOOK IT TO A MUSEUM WHERE THEY TOLD HIM THE WRITING WAS IN LATIN AND SAID THAT FRANCIS DRAKE HAD NAMED THIS PLACE 'PORT DISCOVERY'.

SMITHSONIAN INSTITUTION

THEY ALSO TOLD HIM THAT IT MUST BE A HOAX BECAUSE FRANCIS DRAKE HADN'T SAILED THAT FAR NORTH.

DONALD BELIEVED THEM AND PUT THE PLATE AWAY IN A TRUNK, ONLY FOR IT TO GET STOLEN BY THIEVES. IT WAS NEVER SEEN AGAIN.

At the time when Donald McDonald (still his real name) found the plate and took it to the museum no one had ever suggested that Drake had sailed that far north. So it was an unlikely thing for him to decide to fake. Did Donald really find proof that Drake had sailed as far as Alaska? If he did perhaps one day that plate will be found again in someone's attic or in a junk shop. Or perhaps some other evidence (another brass plate or maybe some English coins) will be discovered in southern Alaska that will solve the mystery and tell us just how far Drake really did get.

New England

We do know that during this period Drake found a location that he thought was rather special…

Drake's Secret Logbook

Ye gads! Today will be long remembered for we have found a place that is perfect for the site of the first English colony in North America. I went on land and claimed the area for good Queen Lizzy. I have named it Nova Albion or 'New England'.

PS What a v. handsome and marvellous fellow I am.

And do we know for sure which bit of North America he actually named Nova Albion?

DO WE HECK!

Wherever Drake had been between May and September 1579 we do know that the next thing he did was sail for home. The only problem, of course, was getting there alive.

THE HOMEWARD BOUNDERS

Drake's only option was going home the long way. With just one ship against all the Spanish in the Pacific, it was far too risky to go south again and try to get back through the Strait of Magellan. It was nearly two years since they had left England, and the crew on the *Golden Hind* had now been reduced to 62 men and boys.

Drake left North America behind him and headed east across the Pacific Ocean. He kept sailing on and on and on and ... well, the Pacific is a pretty BIG ocean, so you get the idea. The *Golden Hind* was at sea for 60 days without sight of any land. Here's how the sailors passed their time when they weren't working...

In late November 1579, the *Golden Hind* reached the Moluccas, a group of islands that used to be called the Spice Islands. The Moluccas are mountainous and covered with thick woods. The natives grew spices like nutmeg, cinnamon, cloves and pepper – all of which cost a small fortune in the west. Here was a good trading opportunity. Or was it?

When the *Golden Hind* was spotted approaching one island, over 100 canoes came out to greet them. Things went a bit pear-shaped, though, when the natives swarmed aboard the *Golden Hind* and started stealing things. The crew just managed to get them off the ship, but the Indians used carefully aimed stones thrown by slingshot as another attack. Finally Drake was forced to use a cannon to blow one of their canoes out of the water, killing about 20 Indians. The *Golden Hind* sailed away still in desperate need of fresh water and food. They were still more than 12,000 miles from the safety of home.

Sultan of spice

Drake and Co had much better luck at the next island. It was ruled by a rather large and (frankly) flabby man called Sultan Babu. Babu had been fighting the Portuguese for many years and, on the basis that 'my enemy's enemy is my friend', he happily gave Drake a grand welcome to the islands. He organized a feast, and Drake's hungry crew were more than happy to devour it.

Several days of trade talks followed, with the result that Babu was presented with a coat of mail, a nice helmet, and a gold ring. In return, Drake got six tons of cloves. Result.

It was also agreed that Drake would return within two years with more English ships and get rid of the Portuguese from the area for good. In return, Babu would give Queen Elizabeth exclusive rights to the very, very, VERY profitable clove trade. Although not well remembered today, when Drake got home the deal with Babu was considered one of his finest achievements.

On the last day of his visit, Drake had the opportunity to do what he enjoyed most – annoy his enemies a bit. Two Portuguese sailors called on Drake assuming him to be Spanish and were surprised and rather alarmed to discover that he was English. To wind them up, Drake told them he had a fleet of 'ten other ships' exploring the area and that he would soon be back with more. The two young captains left in a state of semi-panic to report to their boss. The next day Drake sailed away and they never saw him again.

We don't know too many details about the rest of the long journey home. Here's what we do know…

Drake's Secret Logbook

27 November

Rejoice! When we get home I will be the richest man in all England. (And then some!) Ha! That'll get me noticed by the Queen and her posh advisors. The Golden Hind is full to bursting with 26 tons of Spanish gold, silver, coins, gems, and now six tons of cloves. We are heading east towards Java.

The hull is once again thick with seaweed, which in these warm waters grows at an insane rate.

15 December

Found a small island to careen the ship on. The entire island is swarming with crabs, each one enough to fully feed four grown men. Since our arrival, the crabs, have taken to climbing trees to escape our cooking pot. The men need rest, so I have divided the crew into two parties. One party works one day, while the other does only night duties. What a fair and kindly Master I am. (And let no one disagree with that!)

1 January 1579

Our third New Year's Day away from the shores of fair England. I see the men's faces when they rest. Like me, they wonder what is happening at home with their wives and families.

PS Must remember to look up my wife's name before we get back.

9 January

Disaster! Sailing at full speed we ran aground on a coral reef. Next morning's high tide failed to lift us off. Was forced to order men to lighten ship. Dumped eight cannons and three tons (!) of cloves overboard. (Shed a tear thinking of all that lost cash!) Did the trick though, and we slid off the reef. Phew. Praise the Lord (and me for thinking of such a brilliant idea)!

They stopped in Java to trade with the natives for water and food. Drake impressed the local raja by showing visitors around the ship and with music from his ship's orchestra. (Who had surely had the longest world tour of any musicians ever!) Drake discovered that two of their casual visitors were in fact Portuguese spies and that a great Portuguese war ship was approaching along the coast towards them. Early next morning, Drake gave the order to sail and the *Golden Hind* started across the Indian Ocean, heading for the Cape of Good Hope (the pointy bit at the bottom of Africa).

It took nearly 60 days to cross the Indian Ocean. Fresh water got so low that Drake had his men spread out some of the ship's spare sails on deck to catch rain water. At one point they were down to having just one pint of water left for every three men onboard. They were two or three days at most from it being curtains for the lot of them when they arrived at the coast of Sierra Leone where fresh supplies of water, oysters and fruit were waiting for them.

A secret stop?

Most of the accounts of Drake's great voyage say that he left Sierra Leone and sailed north straight back to England. There is some evidence, however, that suggests that on his way home Drake had a sneaky stop off on the coast of France. One report says that Drake *'brought a great quantity of treasure of gold and silver and unloaded it secretly on Belle Isle and then transported it to the mainland of France.'*

Why would Drake hide some of his treasure in France? Well, perhaps he thought of it as an insurance policy. If he was out of favour in England for any reason (like aggravating the King of Spain too much or for beheading Thomas Doughty) then perhaps Drake thought having a little treasure buried abroad was a rather good idea.

We don't know for sure that he did hide any of the treasure – or if he did, if he ever returned to collect it. It's a nice thought that perhaps it's still out there somewhere waiting to be found.

And home again

Everyone agrees that when Drake first reached home there was only one question on his lips. (And no, it wasn't about his wife. We'll catch up on what she'd been up to in a bit.) Drake's question was about Queen Elizabeth.

Drake had no Internet or television to give him news while he'd been away and, after three long years, nearly anything could have happened in England. The Queen could have made peace with the King of Spain (which would be very bad news for our boy indeed). Or she could have been thrown off her throne, or worst of all, she could have died.

Drake stood on the deck of the *Golden Hind* watching the ships and houses of Plymouth Harbour grow nearer and nearer. After a world-circling voyage of nearly 40,000 miles, they were home. But what kind of a welcome awaited the returning heroes?

As the battered and seaworn *Golden Hind* passed into Plymouth Harbour, Drake spotted some fishermen repairing their nets on the quayside. He cleared his throat and called out one simple question:

'Is the Queen still alive?'

If they said 'no' Drake knew he would probably lose his head.

DRAKE IN COMMAND

When Drake sailed the *Golden Hind* into Plymouth harbour on 28 September 1580, news of his return spread like wildfire. Drake had been away so long that everyone had given him up for dead. Arriving out of nowhere with the largest horde of captured Spanish treasure the world had ever seen made Drake an instant celebrity and all-round English hero.

Local legend (which may or may not be true – you decide) tells how Drake rewarded the fisherman who told him the Queen WAS still alive and kicking by buying him a suit tailored from white silk.

Everyone deciding that you must be dead can cause problems. One of the first things Drake found out after landing at Plymouth was that Mrs Drake, thinking he was lost at sea, had taken up with another gentleman friend. Drake wasn't very happy. He forgave her though.

(Perhaps the fact that her gentleman friend had since died and left her a small fortune helped?)

The first official word from Queen Elizabeth was that she was displeased that Drake had stolen so much treasure from her good mate, the King of Spain. This may well have been just the official line to avoid aggravating King Philip, and before long Elizabeth sent her personal word to Drake that all was well and called him to London.

Drake loaded a little sample of his treasure-trove on to horses and set off for the capital with an armed escort. By the time he reached London, the whole city was buzzing with news of the returning sea captain.

Drake arrived at the royal palace and was received by the Queen. She was eager to hear of his adventures and his success against her enemies. Their meeting lasted over six hours and you can be sure that Drake wasn't in a modest mood.

Drake gave the queen *'a diary of everything that had happened during the three-year voyage as well as a very large chart.'* Her majesty was extremely impressed. Drake had performed an amazing feat: he was the first commander in history to successfully pilot a ship around the world – an amazing voyage of nearly 40,000 miles.

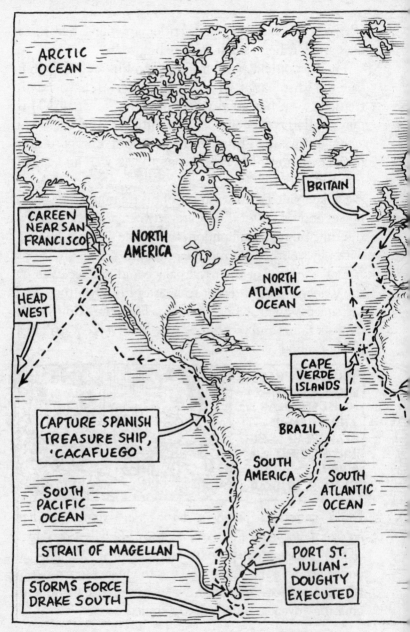

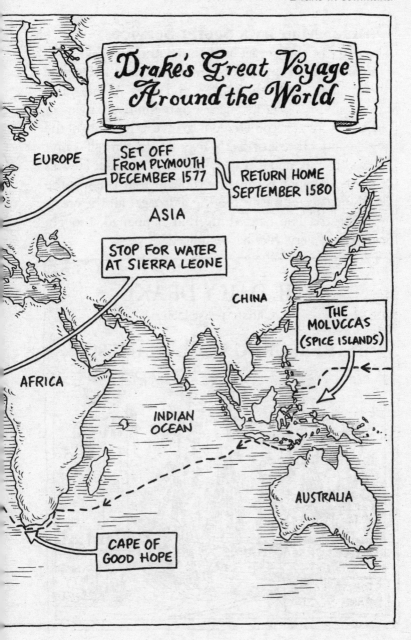

Drake's Great Voyage Around the World

EUROPE

ASIA

SET OFF FROM PLYMOUTH DECEMBER 1577

RETURN HOME SEPTEMBER 1580

STOP FOR WATER AT SIERRA LEONE

CHINA

THE MOLUCCAS (SPICE ISLANDS)

AFRICA

INDIAN OCEAN

AUSTRALIA

CAPE OF GOOD HOPE

On Her Majesty's Secret Service

The diary of the voyage and the map that Drake gave Elizabeth were kept under careful lock and key at the royal palace. Only the Queen and a few of her most trusted advisors ever had access to them. Every member of Drake's crew was ordered not to reveal the route of the voyage under threat of death. Even Drake himself wasn't allowed to talk about it as freely as he wanted. He was probably unhappy because he thought that keeping the details *that* secret meant that he didn't get all the credit he deserved. The next thing that happened, though, made Drake very, very happy indeed.

THE DAILY DRAKE
Christmas Eve 1580

TREASURE ON THE THAMES!

Londoners flocked to the banks of the Thames today to stare with open mouths as Sir Francis Drake sailed his treasure-laden ship, the *Golden Hind*, into the city.

Unofficial sources put the total weight of gold and silver brought home by the dashing Captain Drake at OVER THIRTY TONS! As one sailor said, 'That should keep us in beer for a while.'

The great treasure trove of riches was taken from the ship under armed guard and then placed in a special vault in the Tower of London.

Of course, some of the treasure never made it as far as the Tower of London. Many pearls and other gemstones were pocketed by our boy and some of the crew. But the investors who had put money up to pay for the voyage in the first place still had a bumper payday! For every pound they had invested, they received nearly 50 pounds back. It's hard to know just how much all the treasure was worth in total but the best guess today is that what Drake had captured was worth around £500,000 (half a million pounds)! That was a fantastic amount of money for those days – equal to around 150 million pounds today. (So you can see why Drake was so popular with the Queen.)

Officially the Queen gave Drake £10,000 for himself. Unofficially he had already helped himself to considerably more than that. The money made Drake one of the wealthiest men in the country and he didn't waste any time in letting people know about it.

Going overboard

There was a tradition in the Queen's court of giving presents to celebrate the New Year. This year, Drake went a bit mad and made sure that the presents were the most spectacular ever. He presented the Queen with a crown containing five mighty emeralds, and a diamond cross worth over 5,000 crowns. The Queen was dead happy and wore her new crown on New Year's Day. Drake also spread gifts around the rest of the court, giving silver plate to many of the councillors and secretaries.

OOH, YOU SHOULDN'T HAVE!

Not everyone was so pleased with Drake's gifts though. He tried to give ten bars of gold to Lord Burghley, a member of the Privy Council, but he refused the gold saying *'he did not know how his conscience would allow him to accept a present from Drake, who had stolen all he had.'* Meow.

A couple of the other super-posh people in the court refused gifts as well. Perhaps they were a bit jealous of Drake's success? The noblemen at court were all in permanent competition with each other for the Queen's attention. Drake's round-the-world voyage had turned him into a superstar. Over the next months he was often singled out by the queen and invited to walk and talk with her. One day they met together NINE separate times.

This was a fantastic time for Drake. The news of his successful voyage around the world had spread across Europe like wildfire. Drake was a sensation.

> ## Drake's Secret Logbook
> ### January 1581
> At last I am rightfully recognized as greatest living Englishman and most admired figure in all the land. (It was bound to happen sooner or later!)
>
> PS Thank the Lord for my natural modesty, or all this attention might go straight to my head.

Drake was immortalized in song, verse, books and broadsheets (a kind of early newspaper). One publication singing his praises was sold under the catchy title of:

In commemoration of the valiant and virtuous-minded gentleman Master Francis Drake with a rejoicing of his happy adventures.

A man of wealth and taste

Now that he was one of the richest men in the country, Sir Francis bought himself somewhere to live. He bought a house in Elbow Lane in London to use as a base when he was visiting the Queen at court and attending to other business in the capital. Down in Devon, he paid £3,400

121

for Buckland Abbey – a magnificent place suitable for someone of Drake's new standing as a national hero. Buckland Abbey was an old church that had been converted into a three-storey house. The purchase also included lots of farm buildings around it, and some stunning orchards.

As if times weren't good enough for Drake, they were about to get even better.

THE GOLDEN HIND WAITED ON THE THAMES, DECKED OUT IN BANNERS FROM BOW TO STERN.

AS THE QUEEN STEPPED ONBOARD DRAKE'S SHIP, ONE OF HER GARTERS SLIPPED DOWN HER LEG.

OOPS

THE FRENCH AMBASSADOR QUICKLY PICKED IT UP AND HANDED IT BACK.

SEIGNEUR DE MARCHAUMONT

LIZZY SLIPPED IT BACK ON AND PROMISED...

I SHALL SEND IT TO YOU AS A SOUVENIR.

CHEEKY MINX!

SOME ON-LOOKERS CROWDED ON TO A MAKESHIFT BRIDGE

HOORAY

HOORAY FOR DRAKE

AND GOD SAVE THE-

SOME OF THEM GOT RATHER WET.

SPLOOSH!!

-QUEEN!

123

As well as being a reward for Drake, knighting him served two purposes for Lizzy. Firstly, it let her show King Philip that Drake (and the others like him) had her support. And secondly, by getting the French ambassador to administer the actual taps on his shoulder, Lizzy was sending out a clear hint that perhaps, maybe, just possibly, England and France might form a new alliance. They didn't of course – as always, Lizzy was just keeping everyone guessing.

More honours

Everyone loves a success and Drake was certainly that. The people of Plymouth had got rather worried when Drake had bought Buckland Abbey, fearing that their most famous citizen was about to leave them. To make sure they kept their association with England's new hero, they made Drake the new Lord Mayor of Plymouth.

As if that wasn't enough, Drake also became a Member of Parliament for the local area. We don't know much about his time as an MP because records are sketchy, but do we know he was an MP for about ten years.

Thanks to his skills as a navigator, seaman and leader, Drake had risen from being a lowly sea-hand to being one of the richest men in the country at the very top of society. Lord Mayor Sir Francis Drake MP was a success. He had made it.

THE DRAGON BREATHES FIRE

Over the next few years, Drake was a victim of his own amazing success. What he wanted to do more than anything was take a fleet of ships back to the Pacific Ocean. During Drake's time away, however, tensions between England and Spain had increased. King Philip had recently added the crown of Portugal to his collection of titles and with it the impressive war fleet of the Portuguese navy. It was an open secret that the King of Spain wanted to invade England. The only real question was when would he try to do it? No surprise, then, that the Queen didn't want Drake to venture far from home.

Drake's Secret Logbook
'Tis a tiresome thing. It is said that the King of Spain fears only one Englishman and his name is Drake.
Quite right of course (he should

> *flipping fear me) but it means that the Queen will not let me sail far from these shores, and another trip around the world is forbidden. Rats!*

Drake put forward various plans to go back to the Pacific Ocean, but the Queen wouldn't hear of it. He also proposed setting up England's very first colony, suggesting they found it on the west coast of North America. That didn't happen either.

Drake's day

To most people in England, Sir Francis Drake was a hero. The writer John Stow recorded that '*In court, town and country his name and fame became admirable in all places. People swarmed daily in the streets to behold him.*' Not everyone agreed, though. There were a lot of different opinions about Drake, depending on who you asked.

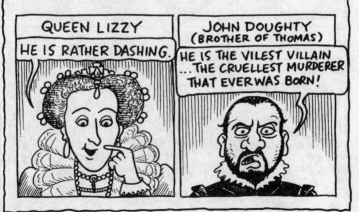

127

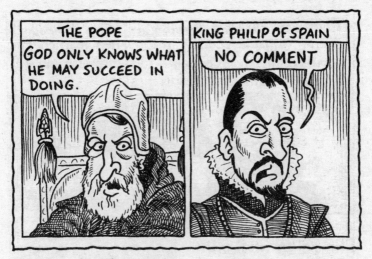

Mary's final voyage

We don't know what she died of, but in January 1583 Drake's wife Mary passed away...

In the year that followed, Drake proposed yet another plan for an expedition to the Pacific. The Queen was still fearful of an all-out war with Spain, but Drake had a clever way of selling the idea to her. He promised that if he went he would stop the flow of gold and silver that was paying for the King of Spain's ships and soldiers. The Queen seemed to go along with the idea for a while but then, as she often did, she changed her mind.

There was soon some good news for Drake, though, at least on personal level. Early in 1585, he remarried. His bride was Elizabeth Sydenham – top posh totty and still in her early twenties. Drake was thrilled.

The reign in Spain

For years, Queen Lizzy had been doing her very best to avoid war with Spain. The main reason was that she was worried about losing. In the summer of 1585, though, the King of Spain overstepped the mark. Here's what he did…

THE DAILY DRAKE
16 June 1585

SNEAKY SPANISH ARREST ENGLISH SHIPS!

Without any warning, King Philip today shocked the world (well, us anyway) by having all English ships in Spanish ports arrested! The war-mongering monarch ordered that everything useful should be stripped from the English ships and put aboard his own Spanish fleet. This vile action is the last straw. War now

---

looks not just inevitable, but like there's no way to avoid it.

The Queen has commissioned top sea-hero Sir Francis Drake to give Spanish bottoms a serious kicking.

THE DAILY DRAKE SAYS: About bally time too!

Drake sailed from Plymouth Harbour with 25 ships loaded with 2,300 sailors and fighting men. Drake's flagship for this adventure was the 600-ton royal naval vessel *Elizabeth Bonaventure*.

Drake's Secret Logbook
14 September 1585
God be praised! Action at last!! Let the Spanish tremble in their boots! Here comes Drake!

The fleet set sail in the middle of September and in something of a rush because Drake was worried that the Queen would change her mind. Here's what happened:

TWO WEEKS LATER, DRAKE AND HIS FLEET SAILED INTO THE PORT OF VIGO WHERE MOST OF THE ENGLISH SHIPS WERE BEING HELD PRISONER.

DRAKE DEMANDED TO KNOW IF ENGLAND AND SPAIN WERE AT WAR. THE SPANISH GOVERNOR GOT RATHER WORRIED RATHER QUICKLY AND AGREED TO RELEASE ALL ENGLISH SHIPS AND SAILORS.

17 NOVEMBER. AFTER STEALING A LOAD OF PROVISIONS FROM THE SPANISH PORT, DRAKE SAILED TO THE CAPE VERDE ISLANDS WHERE HE BURNT SEVERAL TOWNS FOR RANSOM. (OBVIOUSLY IT WAS A QUIET AFTERNOON.)

DRAKE ORDERED THE FLEET TO HEAD ACROSS THE ATLANTIC, BUT AS THEY SAILED A TERRIBLE PLAGUE SPREAD THROUGH THEIR SHIPS, KILLING HUNDREDS OF MEN.

THE FLEET ARRIVED AT SANTA DOMINGO — A LARGE SPANISH FORTRESS-CITY ON HISPANIOLA ISLAND. THE SPANISH BELIEVED THEIR SEA DEFENCES WERE UNBEATABLE (DRAKE DIDN'T).

DRAKE UNEXPECTEDLY LANDED HIS FORCES ON A BEACH THE SPANISH WRONGLY BELIEVED WAS PROTECTED BY ROUGH TIDES. WITHIN HOURS THE TOWN WAS IN DRAKE'S CONTROL.

KING PHILIP AND THE SPANISH ARMY WERE HUMILIATED AGAIN.

DRAKE!

Drake's original orders from the Queen were to free English ships trapped in the port of Vigo and then to attack any towns he fancied on the coast of Spain. Typically, Drake had decided that this was much too modest a plan and he had made up his mind to cross the Atlantic and attack ports on the Spanish Caribbean. Drake thought they would be poorly defended. He was right.

Santo Domingo was the original base of Spanish control in the Caribbean and to have it fall to the English so easily was considered shameful. One report described Drake as attacking the town with *'the ferocity of a demon'*.

To make matters worse (or better – depending whose side you were on) Drake and his men captured a banner which had the King of Spain's motto on it – 'Non Suffict Orbis' or 'The World is Not Enough'. It was extremely embarrassing that the King's own banner had fallen into English hands. Some Spanish officials tried to buy it back from Drake, but he wasn't having any of it.

After a month's stay at Santo Domingo, Drake and his fleet left (taking several captured ships with them) and headed towards the coast of South America.

Drake's next target, the port of Cartagena, barely put up any more of a fight than Santo Domingo had. One witty local said that Drake had threatened to write to the King of Spain to complain about how useless his defences were. (He didn't.)

Disease was still a problem though, and Drake was losing men to illness on a daily basis. While the fleet was occupying the town, discipline went downhill quickly with bored sailors looting and running wild.

The fleet left Cartagena in the middle of April, and after a brief stop at San Agustin...

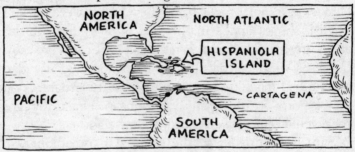

...for a quiet afternoon of looting and burning, the fleet headed north. Drake had heard rumours of an attack on Roanoke and wanted to head it off.

Drake's day

Remember Drake's idea of an English colony on the west coast of North America? Well, no one had fancied going quite that far, but the previous year top English brain-box Sir Walter Raleigh had helped found England's very first colony abroad on Roanoke Island on the nearer east coast of America.

So how had things gone for the colony in the first year? Well…

After one of Drake's ships was sunk by a bad storm with *'hailstones the size of hen's eggs'*, the colonists decided to call it a day and come home with him.

Drake's fleet crossed the Atlantic in about a month and arrived back in Portsmouth at the end of July to a triumphant welcome. The voyage had been a mixture of failure and success. Drake had lost over 700 men from the 2,300 that had set out. Nearly all of them had been killed by disease.

Unlike his round-the-world voyage, this expedition had failed to make money for its investors – in fact they made a small loss. But there was very good news for the Queen and for England because, thanks to Drake, the King of Spain had lost battles, he had lost ships, he had lost men, and he had lost money. Paying for his armies was costing King Philip a fortune, and he could barely afford these new losses. Drake had taken the wind right out of his sails.

Even worse was the fact that his reputation was suffering. Rumours began circulating that the King of Spain was about to go bankrupt. People all over Europe were beginning to see Drake's raids as blows against the King. It was getting personal.

For the average Englishman the main talking point of the voyage was Drake's daringly brilliant attack on Santo Domingo which it was said had *'inflamed the whole country with a desire to adventure on the sea'*.

The clouds of war

At the Queen's request, Drake briefly visited Holland to see Dutch allies who might help in a future fight with the Spanish. He soon returned home. By early in 1587, it was becoming clear to everyone that England and Spain were squaring up for an almighty punch up.

English spies on the continent reported that the Spanish were assembling what they called a grand 'armada' at several Spanish harbours so they could invade England and throw Queen Lizzy off the throne. Urgent action was needed and what followed was probably Drake's single most brilliant naval manoeuvre of his life.

No one knew exactly how ready the Spanish fleet was or when they were going to leave the harbour. Drake was dispatched in the *Elizabeth Bonadventure* with 24 other ships (and 3,000 men) to do as much damage as he could.

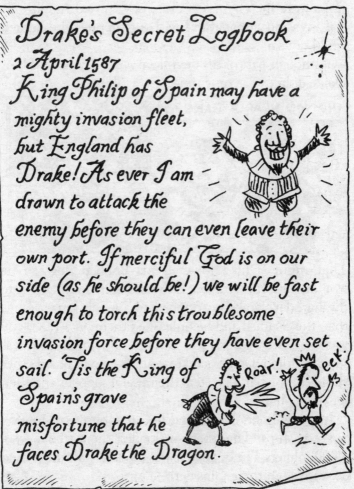

Drake's Secret Logbook
2 April 1587
King Philip of Spain may have a mighty invasion fleet, but England has Drake! As ever I am drawn to attack the enemy before they can even leave their own port. If merciful God is on our side (as he should be!) we will be fast enough to torch this troublesome invasion force before they have even set sail. 'Tis the King of Spain's grave misfortune that he faces Drake the Dragon.

Roar!

eek!

Drake was indeed fast enough and reached Spain before any of the armada had set sail. Drake first approached Lisbon but decided that it was too well protected to attack directly. A couple of local sailors, however, told Drake that there was a large fleet in the harbour at Cadiz. Drake recognized this as the perfect target. Most of the ships were merchant vessels. They carried supplies for the invasion armada and without supplies the armada could not sail.

Although part of his own fleet was a day behind him, Drake didn't waste any time.

That night, Drake lowered his English flags so he wouldn't be spotted too early and sailed straight into the harbour. Drake's cannons had a much longer range than the Spanish and he unleashed them on a 1,000-ton warship. The Spanish ship put up a brief fight, but was soon captured. Drake quickly sent his men to board other vessels in the harbour, steal their useful supplies and then set them alight.

In a few hours Drake and his crew burnt or stole 38 Spanish ships. The Spanish flooded the harbour with 6,000 soldiers, but by then it was too late – all they could do was watch their ships burn.

...smoke and flames rose up so that it seemed like a huge volcano

Drake left the harbour a smouldering ruin and took his fleet south along the coast. Over the next month, Drake and his fleet captured an amazing total of 47 merchant ships, each one loaded with supplies heading for the armada. Drake took particular care to destroy all metal hoops (they were used to make barrels) reasoning that the armada could not sail without supplies of fresh water.

An ambassador in Madrid recorded that...

The English are masters of the sea and hold it at their discretion.

After losing some men to the usual outbreak of a bit of plague, Drake headed to the Azores. They soon spotted a large ship trying to hide in a bay of an island and approached it with cannons ready. After a short exchange of cannon fire, the other captain surrendered.

They had captured a huge Portuguese ship, called the *San Felipe*. She was loaded with spice, jewels and silk, as well as the usual gold and silver. Even better, the *San Felipe* belonged personally to the King of Spain. Drake sailed her back to England with the rest of his fleet and other captured vessels arriving home in Plymouth on 26 June.

The voyage had been a great success. Drake had achieved his military objectives and had managed to steal a darn good horde of treasure too. Drake had put back the attempted invasion by at least a year, but the danger had not gone away. King Philip's plan to add the throne of England to his collection would not be stopped so easily. There were greater dangers ahead for Queen Lizzy and for Drake.

INVASION!

Our boy Drake was keen to refit and re-equip his fleet and head back to the Spanish coast as soon as possible for a second run of attacks. The Queen however wanted to quit while she was ahead and forbid the idea. It was now the autumn of 1587, and with winter gales on the way the English Channel would be too rough to risk any large invasion fleet.

Queen Lizzy was as tight as ever and decommissioned her ships – which meant keeping them in port with no crew onboard – thus saving around £5,000 (a tidy sum) in wages over the winter months. Over in Spain, King Philip licked his wounds and renewed his preparations. Drake, Queen Lizzy and England itself had become thorns in his side that had to be dealt with.

AND IT ALSO MEANS SAVING THREE SHILLINGS ON SHIP'S BISCUITS...

Drake's day

Remember when those sneaky Spanish attacked Drake and John Hawkins in San Juan? (see page 28) Well, when John Hawkins had got home he had to explain to Her Majesty exactly why some English ships had escaped while other hadn't. He soon realized that the secret lay in their design.

While Drake had been off gallivanting around the world, John Hawkins had been at home working hard on making improvements to the design of British ships.

Drake had a new ship for the forthcoming battle against the Spanish. It was the 400-ton *Revenge* and it included all the improvements that Hawkins had developed:

TOPSAILS TO CATCH MORE WIND AND ADD TO SPEED

LOWER 'CASTLES' AT BOW AND STERN SO LESS WIND RESISTANCE

GUN PORTS TO ALLOW CANNONS TO FIRE FROM THE LOWER DECKS. KEEPING CANNONS LOWER IN THE SHIP ADDED TO ITS STABILITY

MORE STREAMLINED HULL FOR GREATER SPEED IN THE WATER

There were other advantages to Hawkins' redesign too. For a start his ships lay lower in the water and so were a smaller target for enemy fire. Hawkins also replaced the old iron cannons (which sometimes exploded) with brass ones that were stronger and less likely to blow up.

Philip the fibber

King Philip was aware that thanks to Drake's raids of the previous summer, England now had plenty of time to prepare for his invasion. He tried upsetting Queen Lizzy's preparations for war by leaking some 'secret' news. Basically, this is what it said:

Dear Sir:

King Philip can't come out to war today 'cos his soldiers are all sick or dead or have run away. So don't worry about organizing your defences and things 'cos you are quite safe.

Yours

~~*King Philip*~~

King Philip's mum

Drake wasn't fooled for a second and he was proved right when the information received turned out to be nonsense. King Philip was pushing ahead with his plans to invade England and the only thing standing in his way was Sir Francis Drake and a fleet of England's finest.

Battle plans

Early in 1588, the Queen and her advisors met to talk strategy and decide what they should do when the armada set sail. The first plan that they came up with didn't go down too well with Drake, and he wrote to tell them so.

Drake's Secret Logbook
April 1588
The Queen (Gawd bless her) and her advisors (idiots!) have come up with a plan so terrible that it would send us all to a watery grave. Their foolish idea is to split the goodly English fleet into two. 'Tis utter madness! If either half met the full armada it would be defeated for certain – allowing the armada to sail on and then defeat the second half. I have written to the Queen to appeal for sanity. Why have they not asked the opinion of England's

> greatest-ever sea captain – me! →
> (Perhaps it is because they think I am
> too shy??) In my view we should once
> again set sail for Spain and fight the
> armada at sea or in their own ports.

A change of plan

In those days, sea commanders thought that it was best to wait for your enemy to come and attack you. Francis Drake and John Hawkins and several other naval bigwigs had come around to the view that if you knew you were going to be attacked then it was best to take the fight to the enemy on your own terms. Drake argued his corner (something he was very good at) and eventually he won the Queen over to his plan. Once she changed her mind, so did everyone else. (And very quickly too.)

As the weeks of spring ticked slowly by, Drake did what he could to prepare for war. He wrote many letters, demanding more and better supplies for his ships and for his men. As he always had on longer sea voyages, he tried to gather as much information as possible too. Word reached Drake from a spy ship off the Spanish coast that the armada was being equipped with English flags for use during battle to confuse the enemy. Drake was outraged.

Chain of command

Now came the point when Queen Lizzy had to decide exactly what rank to give Drake. The person in charge of England's navy was Lord Howard. There was no way that Drake could be given command above him. For one thing, although Drake was a great sea men, he wasn't too good at working in a team. Also, many navy officers who considered Drake an upstart and no more than a common pirate wouldn't stand for it. On the other hand, Drake was a proud man, and both he and the Queen knew that as far as the Spanish were concerned, Drake WAS the English navy.

Drake was summoned to a meeting with the Queen and told that he was to be Lord Howard's second-in-command with the title of Vice Admiral. Any disagreement between the two men would cost England very dearly in the battles to come – just as well, then, that the two men hit it off like a house on fire. With both of them going out of the way to praise the other, the English were united together against their common foe.

The armada sets sail

Drake had just about persuaded everyone to go for his plan of attacking the armada BEFORE it set sail, when it er … set sail. Everyone apart from Drake had wasted too much time talking about what to do instead of doing it. As luck would have it, the Spanish didn't get far before the armada hit gale-force winds that swept the ships south, AWAY from England. Drake and Howard ordered their own fleet to set sail, but as they tried to reach the Spanish armada they too were overcome by storms. They were all getting nowhere fast.

A load of old bowls

Now we get to one of the most famous legends about Drake. It might be true, it might not be true – you decide. The story goes that on 19 July 1588, news arrived in

Plymouth that the armada had been spotted off the coast of Cornwall. At the time, Drake was playing bowls and legend has it that he turned to his fellow commanders and said…

It's said that Drake knew that the tide was against them and he knew that the English ships could not leave harbour for another few hours, but it makes a lovely story anyway.

So what were the Spanish up to?

The Spanish battle plan went something like this… The armada – with 8,000 sailors and 19,000 soldiers spread over 130 ships – would sail through the English Channel, sinking anyone stupid enough to get in their way. Then the armada would meet up off the Flemish coast (Belgium to you and me) where the Duke of Parma had another 27,000 soldiers waiting. The armada would then escort Parma's men across the Channel and they'd all land in Kent together. Then the plan was to beat the English, and march to London to claim the crown before teatime.

The battle fleets

After years of being on the edge of war, the two fleets of
Spain and England were finally about to face each other in
the greatest sea battle the world had ever seen. Here's how
the two fleets shaped up…

Spanish Fleet (Under the command of Medina Sidonia)

No of ships: 130
Strengths: Better at close combat like grappling and boarding. Large numbers of manly
soldiers for hand-to-hand combat. Armada commanders were experienced in battle.
Weaknesses: Slower than English ships, and not as manoeuvrable.
Tactics: Get close to English ships and allow soldiers to swarm over them.

English Fleet:

No of ships: 120
Strengths: English cannons had better aim and considerably further range than the Spanish. The English also had more experience at using heavy guns at sea. Thanks to Hawkins' redesign, English ships were now faster and quicker to manoeuvre.
Weaknesses: English sailors better at er ... sailing than fighting.
Tactics: Keep enemy at a distance and pound them with heavy cannon fire. Aim for near the waterline and try and sink them.

THE REVENGE

Let battle commence

The English ships had trouble getting out of their harbour because they were running against the tide and the wind. They sent out small boats ahead of them to drop anchor and then pulled the ship out using the anchor cable. It was very hard work.

> ### Drake's Secret Logbook
> 19 July
> This is it! It has finally come to all-out war - me (with a bit of help from the English navy) versus the King of Spain. What happens in the next few days will decide England's fate for ever. May the Lord have mercy upon us all. (And a bit of wind wouldn't go amiss either.) Watch out you shifty Spaniards - here I come!

BY THE AFTERNOON OF 20 JULY 54 ENGLISH SHIPS HAD GOT OUT TO SEA

HERE WE GO, HERE WE GO...

THE SPANISH ARMADA WAS IN A TIGHTLY PACKED CRESCENT-FORMATION TWO MILES WIDE

COME AND HAVE A GO IF YOU THINK YOU'RE HARD ENOUGH...

Drake's Secret Logbook
2 AM, 21 July

The fleet is working its way westward in the darkness. The wind has shifted and we may be able to get behind the Spanish line by dawn.

NEXT MORNING THE SPANISH FIND THAT THE ENGLISH ARE AT THEIR REAR. (NOT A COMFORTABLE POSITION FOR THEM)

DRAKE SAILED THE REVENGE DANGEROUSLY CLOSE TO THE RIGHT WING OF THE SPANISH CRESCENT AND EXCHANGED SHOTS.

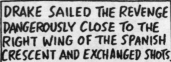

FOR THREE HOURS, THE ENGLISH FLEET FIRED EVERY CANNON THEY HAD, BUT THEY INFLICTED LITTLE DAMAGE.

AT 5 PM, A HUGE EXPLOSION RIPPED THROUGH THE SPANISH SHIP, THE SAN SALVADOR, AS ITS GUNPOWDER STORE BLEW UP.

WUMPH!

Drake's Secret Logbook

Wind has driven the Spanish fleet east along the English Channel. I have orders to lead the fleet through the night by placing a lantern on the ship's stern to act as a beacon. Around 3 am I extinguished the lantern to go and investigate an unknown vessel and ended up capturing the Rosario - one of the armada's pay ships. (Must remember not to rub my hands together in glee in front of Lord Howard. He might not be too keen on me leaving the battle to capture a bit more cash for myself!)

DRAKE'S REVENGE EXECUTES A STUNNING SEA MOVE, UNLEASHING NOT ONE, BUT TWO BROADSIDES AGAINST THE SPANISH GRAN GRIFON.

The English fleet continued to shadow the armada as they moved east down the English Channel. On Saturday 27 July, at around six in the evening, the armada reached Calais on the French coast. Drake and Lord Howard watched as the Spanish armada made anchor there. What they did next would decide the fate of England.

ON THE ROCKS

It was all starting to look a bit dodgy for the Spanish. The commander of the armada, Medina Sidonia, sent several messages to the Duke of Parma asking him where and when the two forces should meet on the Flemish coast. After several unanswered messages, the Duke of Parma finally replied that he wouldn't be ready for another week.

This was not good news for the Spanish. It meant that the armada was expected to stay in the English Channel fighting off the wind, tides, weather *and* the English fleet all that time.

Light my fire

On the morning of Sunday 28 July, Lord Howard and Drake called a council of war. The Spanish were vulnerable, but ONLY if they could be made to move out of the relative safety of where they were now anchored.

English ships could, of course, just sail in and attack, but the situation greatly favoured the Spanish who, Drake thought, would prove hard to dislodge. The answer came from Sir William Winter, a captain on one of the ships that had just arrived to join the fleet…

THAT NIGHT, EIGHT MERCHANT SHIPS WERE PACKED WITH MATERIALS THAT WOULD BURN EASILY AND THEIR CANNONS WERE LOADED READY TO FIRE.

THE CREWLESS SHIPS WERE POINTED AT THE SPANISH FLEET 'SAFE' AT ANCHOR.

THEN THEY WERE SET ON FIRE.

THE FIRESHIPS CAUSED PANIC IN THE SPANISH FLEET, WITH THEIR CAPTAINS DESPERATE TO GET OUT OF THE WAY.

The fireships did not set fire to a single Spanish ship, but they had more than done their job. The Spanish armada had been dislodged from its safe haven and was now at the mercy of winds, tides and the English fleet. The armada was no longer the carefully organized fleet that had been able to keep the English at bay.

Drake's Secret Logbook

29 July

Praise the Lord! (And me a bit, too!) What a day! With the Spanish out of their safe harbour and scattered, we had our chance. My squadron of ships (led by me in the Revenge of course) moved in to take on the Spanish flagship, the San Martin. We fired the first shots in the Battle of

Gravelines (which lasted nine hours!) The San Martin was hit by over 100 cannon shots.

The fighting was so intense between the two fleets that smoke from the cannon fire made it impossible to see more than a few metres.

At one point a cannon ball blasted its way through the captain's cabin on Drake's ship. Drake and two others survived the cannon ball's entry and exit – although it was recorded that the cannon ball passed through *'taking off the toes of one who was there with them.'* Ouch.

The Spanish came off much worse during the exhausting nine-hour battle. Two Spanish ships were beached by their captains (meaning that they were run aground so that the crew could escape alive). The *Maria Juan* was badly hit and suddenly sank with most of her crew. The battle had gone well for the English. So well that Drake himself wrote: *'God hath given us so good a daye.'*

The English fleet shadowed the Spanish overnight without engaging them. The next morning Medina Sidonia decided to launch one more attack. He wanted to bring the English ships into a battle at close quarters where the Spanish soldiers might overwhelm the English crews.

Sidonia fired his signal gun to order the rest of the armada into battle. Only about a dozen Spanish ships obeyed his order – the rest ignored him. Furious, Sidonia had the signal gun fired again. Most of his fleet still refused to respond. Now seething with rage, Sidonia finally got the armada together and sentenced 20 of his disobedient captains to hang! (Only one actually was, though.)

It was the end...

THE DAILY DRAKE
2 August 1588

VICTORY!
England 1 — Spain 0

Thanks to that dashing Drake, we've won!! And what a victory. Not a single English ship was lost. England is safe from those pesky Spaniards and Her Majesty's royal bottom is still safely on her throne. The Spanish armada is bruised, battered, beaten and heading home with its tail between its legs.

THE DAILY DRAKE
SAYS — Well done lads!

The English fleet headed home as well. A lot of ships had been badly damaged by Spanish cannon fire and needed urgent repair. Supplies of food and fresh water were growing low, and even worse, plague was once again running rife through many of the ships, killing thousands of men. Lord Howard wrote to the Queen saying '…*in some vessels so many men are sick that the ships could not weigh anchor. They sicken one day and die the next.*'

The wreck of the armada

If the English sailors seemed to be having a hard time of it, that was nothing compared to what the Spanish were going through. The battered armada began to make its way home around the top of Scotland and along the Irish coast. The English had sunk about ten ships and many of the surviving vessels were barely able to keep afloat. So many Spanish sailors had been killed that there were hardly enough to crew the ships properly. They were also running out of food fast.

As they rounded the Scottish coast, two powerful storms hit the armada, sinking several ships. As the battle-damaged fleet made its way down the coast of Ireland, ship after ship became wrecked. Perhaps the unluckiest man in the entire fleet was Alonso de Leyva. Here's what happened to him...

• Alonso de Leyva avoids cannon balls, musket shot and fireshipss during battle with English.
• While sailing onboard the *Rata Coronada* he is wrecked on the Irish coast, saved and taken onboard the *Duquesa Santa Ana*.
• While sailing onboard the *Duquesa Santa Ana* he's wrecked on the Irish coast, saved and taken onboard the *Girona*.
• While sailing onboard the *Girona*, he is wrecked on the Irish coast. This time the thrice-wrecked Alonso goes down with the ship. Glug. Glug.

Back in England

Lizzy had gone to visit her army, who were waiting at Tilbury in Essex in case the Duke of Parma made it across the Channel with his troops.

I'm still washing my hair.

Lizzy gave a stirring speech to the troops that included the famous bit:

I know I have the body of a weak and feeble woman, but I have the heart and stomach of a king, and a king of England too – and think foul scorn that Parma or any prince of Europe should dare to invade the borders of my realm…

News, even of really important things like battles, could take a good couple of weeks to reach even the Queen.

THE TIME IS 5:45 AND HERE ARE THE CLASSIFIED BATTLE RESULTS...

In reality the armada was finished, but as Europe held its breath and waited to hear news of the battle, an extraordinary rumour began to spread. It may have started because after the armada fled, the English fleet split up into small groups and put into different ports. Anyone seeing them returning might have thought that whichever small group they were looking at was ALL of the English fleet that was left.

Whatever the cause, the very naughty Spanish ambassador in Paris, Don Bernardino de Mendoza, began telling everyone who would listen (which was everyone) that the Spanish had sunk 25 English galleons and had captured Sir Francis Drake and made him a prisoner onboard the Spanish flagship.

Meddling Mendoza went as far as to light a victory bonfire in the middle of Paris. (So not trying to show off at all then.) The truth soon caught up with him, though, and his humiliation was complete when his 'report' was published in England under the title 'A Pack of Spanish Lies'.

Counting the cost

In reality, the armada had been an absolute utter disaster for Spain. The armada had set sail with 130 ships and with high hopes. It had limped back to Spain with about half that number, the rest lost. Out of those that did get home, another dozen ships were no good for anything except firewood. Over 11,000 Spanish soldiers had died. The King of Spain said that he would have another go next year, but no one really believed him. The threat to invade England was over.

LAST VOYAGES

As it became clear just how badly the Spanish armada had been defeated, the Queen and her advisors began to wonder if they should try and finish off King Philip for once and for all. There were two possible options. They could send ships to the coast of Spain and attack the survivors of the armada there, or they could send ships to intercept and capture the next Spanish treasure fleet coming across the Atlantic.

Drake and Lord Howard weren't keen on either idea.

I'M NOT SURE WE'RE ENTIRELY READY.

Here's how Drake saw the situation…

Drake's Secret Logbook
August 1588
As usual it is up to me to talk some
goodly common sense to the rest of
them. Off to London to explain to the
Queen and her advisors (fools!) that
her navy is ever so slightly exhausted.
Before the fleet can put to sea again
we must first cure the spreading
sickness, then help our injured seamen,
and then repair our damaged ships.
Some of the Queen's advisors speak of
'just' sailing to the Azores as if it were
an evening out at a fancy play. Land
lubbers! Our sailors have done
England a great service (as have I!)
and they need time to recover.

Drake had never dodged a fight in his life, but he and
Lord Howard knew that what the English fleet needed
was time to repair and recover, not another military
mission. Drake and Howard got their way, not least
because no one could quite decide what to do next. One
Spanish spy in London reported to his spymaster that *'So
many rumours are current that it is impossible to know how
much to believe.'*

Scene stealer

On 9 September 1588 a young upstart explorer called Thomas Cavendish arrived back in Plymouth, having sailed right around the world and stolen lots of Spanish treasure. Sound familiar? Just to rub salt in the wound, a couple of months later Cavendish sailed his ship, *Desire*, up the Thames as crowds of Londoners cheered him on. Of course Drake was a good sport about it all...

The Secret Logbook of
Sir Francis 'Furious' Drake

Bah humbug! The entire city has gone mad and has thrown itself at the feet of that tiresome copycat show-off Cavendish. What's he got that I haven't got? (Except youth and good looks.) Not only is he stealing my thunder, but he has openly disagreed with my discovery that there are islands at the southern tip of South America.[4] Just who does he think he is?

I wish the Queen (Gawd bless her majesty) would stop insisting on so much secrecy and let me publish the full story of my voyage and discoveries. Then everyone could see who's really top sea dog. (Me!)

---

[4] Drake was right, Cavendish was wrong. Score one for our boy!

Towards the end of 1588, Drake found that he was spending so much time in London that he decided to buy a house close to the river Thames in town. The house had been a royal residence many years before, and was suitably flash for England's most famous mariner.

In the spring of 1589 Drake had something to smile about when Parliament commissioned a special silver medallion to commemorate his voyage around the globe.

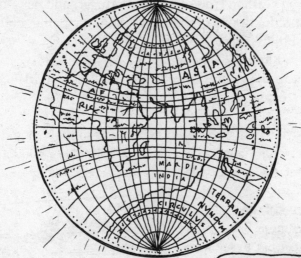

The medallion showed a map of the world with the route sailed by Drake marked out with a dotted line. It was the first time that a map of the world had been published in England.

CAVENDISH HASN'T GOT ONE OF THESE!

Mission impossible

Queen Lizzy finally made up her mind as to what she wanted the English navy to do next. Remember there were quite a few options? Well, Lizzy decided that she wanted to do *all* of them.

This was her wish list:

1 Sail to Spain and destroy the rest of the armada (currently being repaired).

2 Invade Lisbon (the capital of Portugal) and put a new king on the throne of Portugal. (Thus removing some of King Philip's power.)

And just for good measure…

3 Sail to the Azores. Invade all the islands and seize all their treasure ships.

As battle plans go, this one was absolutely bonkers. Here's what happened to the 180 ships and 17,000 men that set out…

Because of the government being tight, the fleet put to sea with only five weeks' worth of food and water.

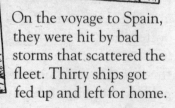

On the voyage to Spain, they were hit by bad storms that scattered the fleet. Thirty ships got fed up and left for home.

The fleet went to attack the harbour where they thought the armada was being repaired … only the harbour was empty. (Oops.)

Just for a change, a terrible disease hit the fleet. (Again.)

The fleet landed men near Lisbon hoping for a revolt in favour of putting a new king on the throne of Portugal. No one cared.

The fleet headed for the Azores, but was beaten back by strong winds.

The fleet arrived back home much the worse for wear.

The capture of a fleet of 60 merchant ships full of naval supplies was about the only good thing that had happened during the entire expedition. Not only had the expedition failed in every single one of its objectives but it had also cost the lives of nearly half the 17,000 men that had set sail.

It was a terrible loss that was almost entirely self-inflected. The men died because of the overambitous and badly thought-out battle plan, and because there wasn't enough food and supplies onboard when the fleet set out.

High and dry

The next bit of Drake's story is a bit fuzzy and no one really knows what happened. There seems to have been some kind of falling-out between Drake and Queen Lizzy. No one knows exactly why. It wasn't unusual – Lizzy was a good queen but she was always getting in a strop with one Lord or another. It could have been over the poor performance of the expedition (although that was far from being all Drake's fault), or perhaps it was something else entirely. Either way, in November 1590 Drake left the royal court and didn't go back for three years.

A man called Richard Hakluyt was preparing a book retelling accounts of great sea voyages and discoveries. He had expected to be able to include the first full account of Drake's voyage (which up to now, much to Drake's annoyance, had been kept secret). At the last minute, though, Hakluyt had to put in a little note to the reader apologizing for not being able to spill the beans about Drake's adventures after all. Was the Queen moody enough with Drake that she stopped his story being told? Possibly.

When it was clear that he was no longer welcome at court, Drake moved from London to live at Buckland Abbey. He split his time between his new duties as Deputy Lord Lieutenant of Devon, and writing an account of his great voyage, hoping that one day it might be published.

Picture this

Drake was getting older. In 1591, our sea hero had achieved the ripe old age of 51, and you have to remember that the average age of death in Drake's day was around 40.

The year after his falling out with the Queen, Drake commissioned the most in-demand portrait painter of the time, Marcus Gheeraerts, to do a picture of him. Portraits of the time always contained more information than just what the subject looked like. Here's how to decode the picture of Drake.

COAT OF ARMS - STARS BECAUSE DRAKE USED THE SKY TO NAVIGATE ON HIS VOYAGES. MOTTO MEANS 'THUS GREAT THINGS ARISE FROM SMALL'.

JEWEL - GIVEN TO HIM BY THE QUEEN AND SHOWING A PICTURE OF HER ROYAL LOVELINESS.

SWORD - DRAKE'S HAND HOVERS BY HIS SWORD INDICATING THAT HE IS A MAN OF ACTION.

GLOBE - SIGNALLING DRAKE WAS AN EXPLORER.

The ice melts

As suddenly as Drake had found himself out of favour, he was back in. Around Christmas 1592, Drake received an invitation to visit the queen and wasted no time in visiting court. By all accounts it was a warm meeting, and very soon afterwards Drake began sending Her Majesty plans and suggestions for a new expedition to the Caribbean. As usual there were a lot of suggestions and counter-suggestions. The Queen was still worried that Spain might launch another attempt to invade England again and wanted her ships and men close to home. Finally she agreed to Drake going, and he set sail in August 1595 (that's two-and-a-half years wasted in talking about it). Drake was sharing command of the fleet of 27 ships with his old shipmate John Hawkins. Hawkins was 63, Drake was 54, and by the standards of the day they were old men. (In fact Drake had written his will just before he sailed, although he took it with him instead of signing it.) Predictably, things did not go well. Here's how Drake might have looked back on the voyage…

Drake's Secret Logbook

23 January 1596

Merciful Lord! We have had nothing but rotten luck from the very start of this voyage. We had so many delays on the journey over that the Spanish were warned we were coming and had their defences ready. (Very unfair! Boo!)

Then, on the very day of our arrival in these waters, my old friend John Hawkins lost his battle with illness and passed away. Seeing him laid to rest made me feel old and lonely. What am I doing out here at my age?

Our night attack on the port itself was beaten back and even when we moved on to other targets we found them well prepared to repel us. This is not like the old days. It has been a woeful voyage and all for naught. To make matters as bad as they could be, the men have now started dying of the fever.

Drake was not long for this world and was soon ill himself with dysentery. For one week he lay in his cabin getting weaker and weaker. It was the end. At three in the morning of 28 January 1596, the greatest sea captain that England has ever known summoned the very last of his strength. He forced himself to get out of bed, and with the help of two of his crew he put on his full body armour. When he was ready for battle, the sailors lowered him carefully down on to his bed once more. Within an hour he was dead.

THE DAILY DRAKE
Special Final Edition

DRAKE IS DEAD!

Shocking news from the Caribbean reached England today that sea captain and all-round dashing hero Sir Francis Drake has passed away, the victim (like so many) of shipboard disease. This is a most grave and terrible loss for England, the country he defended and loved so well.

The entire English fleet came to anchor to attend Drake's burial service. As trumpets played and cannons boomed their final goodbye, Drake's lead coffin was allowed to slip gently into the ocean to disappear beneath the waves. England's greatest hero is gone. (Sob!)

The news was received with rather different reactions in England and Spain. Basically, it went like this…

Whether it was by the English or the Spanish, Drake's name would never ever be forgotten.

Well done, Drake

After his death, Drake became an instant legend. Tributes celebrating Drake and his adventures were everywhere – in songs, poems, stories, and broadsheets. About 30 years after Drake died, two books were published that told his story: *Sir Francis Drake Revived* and *The World Encompassed by Sir Francis Drake*. They became bestsellers. These two books retold Drake's story for a new generation and kept his legend alive.

In his lifetime, Drake rose from humble beginnings to become the most famous sea captain of his age. What Drake did changed the course of history. His raids against the Spanish helped keep Queen Lizzy on the throne, and his fearsome reputation helped ensure the defeat of the Spanish armada. He showed that England's navy was second best to no one and inspired English sea captains for centuries to come.

As a human being, Drake showed different parts of his character to different people. He could be smart, cunning and utterly fearless in battle, unpredictable, strict, greedy and vain.

Drake's old home, Buckland Abbey in Devon, is open to the public. On display there in the Drake Gallery is an instrument known as Drake's Drum, said to be the one that our boy took on many of his voyages, including the defeat of the Spanish armada. No one is quite sure if the drum really is one that Drake owned, but legends say that when England is in mortal danger then the drum sounds an eerie beat as a warning to summon Sir Francis Drake back to protect England once more.

Four hundred years after he first set sail, Sir Francis Drake – master pirate, sea captain, gentleman and rogue – is still Horribly Famous, which is *exactly* how he would have wanted it.